Job Satisfaction of School-Based Speech-Language Pathologists

This text responds to the growing need for speech-language pathologists in school settings by asking how factors including people, work, pay, opportunities for promotion, and supervision impact the overall job satisfaction of school-based speech-language pathologists.

Drawing on data from a quantitative study conducted in schools in the USA, the text foregrounds the experiences and perspectives of speech-language pathologists working in the public-school sector, and illustrates the critical role of effective and supportive educational leadership and administration in ensuring effective recruitment, retention, and job satisfaction among these much-needed professionals. The text highlights growing responsibilities of speech-language pathologists in schools and considers how recruitment and challenges in the sector can be remedied by a greater understanding of how job satisfaction relates to speech-language pathologists' experiences and perspectives on pay, work, opportunities for promotion, and support from a supervisor.

This short text is aimed at researchers, scholars, and administrators in meeting the growing needs of children and students with speech and language difficulties in early childhood, elementary, and secondary education settings. The text will be particularly valuable for school leaders looking to support speech-language pathologists in their setting.

Kimberly A. Boynton is a certified Speech Language Pathologist and Assistant Professor in the Department of Speech Language Pathology at Saint Mary's College, Notre Dame, Indiana, USA.

Routledge Research in Special Educational Needs

This series provides a forum for established and emerging scholars to discuss the latest debates, research and practice in the evolving field of Special Educational Needs.

Books in the series include:

Understanding the Voices and Educational Experiences of Autistic Young People
From Research to Practice
Craig Goodall

Adult Interactive Style Intervention and Participatory Research Designs in Autism
Bridging the Gap between Academic Research and Practice
Lila Kossyvaki

The Global Convergence of Vocational and Special Education
Mass Schooling and Modern Educability
John G. Richardson, Jinting Wu, and Douglas M. Judge

Families Creating Employment Opportunities for Individuals with Developmental Disabilities
Understanding the Contribution of Familial Entrepreneurship
Jennifer Percival

Job Satisfaction of School-Based Speech-Language Pathologists
Insights to Inform Effective Educational Leadership
Kimberly A. Boynton

For more information about this series, please visit: www.routledge.com/Routledge-Research-in-Special-Educational-Needs/book-series/RRSEN

Job Satisfaction of School-Based Speech-Language Pathologists
Insights to Inform Effective Educational Leadership

Kimberly A. Boynton

NEW YORK AND LONDON

First published 2021
by Routledge
605 Third Avenue, New York, NY 10158

and by Routledge
2 Park Square, Milton Park, Abingdon, Oxon, OX14 4RN

Routledge is an imprint of the Taylor & Francis Group, an informa business

© 2021 Kimberly A. Boynton

The right of Kimberly A. Boynton to be identified as author of this work has been asserted by her in accordance with sections 77 and 78 of the Copyright, Designs and Patents Act 1988.

All rights reserved. No part of this book may be reprinted or reproduced or utilised in any form or by any electronic, mechanical, or other means, now known or hereafter invented, including photocopying and recording, or in any information storage or retrieval system, without permission in writing from the publishers.

Trademark notice: Product or corporate names may be trademarks or registered trademarks, and are used only for identification and explanation without intent to infringe.

Library of Congress Cataloging-in-Publication Data
Names: Boynton, Kimberly A., author.
Title: Job satisfaction of school-based speech-language pathologists : insights to inform effective educational leadership / Kimberly A. Boynton Ph.D., CCC-SLP.
Description: New York : Routledge, 2021. | Includes bibliographical references and index.
Identifiers: LCCN 2021001591 (print) | LCCN 2021001592 (ebook) | ISBN 9780367565848 (Hardback) | ISBN 9781003098492 (eBook)
Subjects: LCSH: Educational leadership. | Speech therapists—Employment—United States. | Job satisfaction.
Classification: LCC LB2806 .B64 2021 (print) | LCC LB2806 (ebook) | DDC 331.12/91616855—dc23
LC record available at https://lccn.loc.gov/2021001591
LC ebook record available at https://lccn.loc.gov/2021001592

ISBN: 978-0-367-56584-8 (hbk)
ISBN: 978-0-367-56585-5 (pbk)
ISBN: 978-1-003-09849-2 (ebk)

Typeset in Times New Roman
by Apex CoVantage, LLC

To my parents, George and the late Mary Weil,
who supported my love of inquiry, teaching, learning,
and researching with immeasurable encouragement
and love.

To my husband, Chris, who values my love
of learning and encourages me to find joy
in each day.

Contents

	Acknowledgments	viii
	Author Bio	ix
1	Introduction	1
2	Understanding Speech-Language Pathology Practice in the Educational Setting	14
3	Understanding Motivating Factors to Support Speech-Language Pathology Job Satisfaction	27
4	School-Based Speech-Language Pathologist Job Satisfaction	36
5	Facet-Based Job Satisfaction	44
6	Professional Experience and Job Satisfaction	77
7	Research to Practice: Considerations for Educational Leaders	84
	Index	91

Acknowledgments

I want to especially acknowledge Dr. Terry McDaniel, Dr. Bradley Balch, and Dr. David Marcotte, who offered advice, feedback, and affirmations at various points during the research process. Your knowledge, guidance, and supportive insight encouraged me to develop my research interests.

Thank you to everyone at Routledge Taylor & Francis Group, including the editors, copyeditors, and all who shared in the work, including Elsbeth, Anna-Mary, and Jessica, who patiently answered all my questions and helped make this monograph a reality with their guidance, insight, and excellent feedback.

I want to thank all the speech-language pathologists who took the time to complete the survey that provided data for this research. The work you do each day is valuable and important for so many students and families. Your ongoing collaborative work with your educational colleagues and families continues to emphasize the goal of supporting students on their education journey. In addition, thank you to all of my colleagues in the field of education. I continue to learn from you and professionally grow as a result of the valuable collaborative discussions we have shared, built on problem-solving, critical thinking, and understanding. I want to thank the administrators and leaders who will read this book and gain insight that will provide context and encouragement for gaining further knowledge of the role of speech-language pathologists and the contributions they can make to your school and district teams.

A heartfelt thank you to my husband, Chris, my best friend—I am truly thankful for your constant support, whether I am experiencing a moment of success or failing forward.

Author Bio

Kimberly A. Boynton, Ph.D., CCC-SLP
Dr. Kimberly Boynton is a certified Speech Language Pathologist holding the ASHA Certificate of Clinical Competence, Indiana Professional Licensing Agency Speech-Language Pathologist license, Indiana Department of Education licensing in the areas of Speech Language Pathology, Director of Exceptional Services, and School Superintendent. She has speech-language pathology experience working with children ages birth to high school in various early childhood education settings, public and private schools, home-based services, and private practice settings. She received a Bachelor of Science degree in Audiological and Speech Sciences and a Master of Science degree in Speech Language Pathology from Purdue University. She received her Director of Exceptional Needs License in 2013 from Ball State University. In 2019, she received her Doctor of Philosophy degree in Educational Administration from Indiana State University. Dr. Boynton has held clinical and administrative positions in the field of education. She has focused work in the area of high-quality early childhood services, including significant work on community level committees and task force groups to support and empower children and families. School-based experience has focused on the provision of speech and language assessment and intervention services, educator professional development, teacher evaluation system implementation, grant writing and management, and development and implementation of early childhood services. Dr. Boynton worked as a Director of Early Childhood Services within a large urban public-school district in Northern Indiana, working collaboratively with community early childhood programs and Head Start. Additionally, she studied and led the implementation of early childhood programming in a large urban public-school district to support the community's need for additional early childhood opportunities for children and families. She has held the position of Coordinator of Early Childhood/Preschool Special Education, working to ensure equitable and appropriate services

for children. Additionally, she is a member of the Elkhart County Source's Reach Out to Connect Kids (ROCK) Team to support the role communication has in behavior and the accessibility for all children to communicate effectively during the early childhood years through supporting classroom educators, children, and families. Current work as an Assistant Professor in the Department of Speech Language Pathology at Saint Mary's College in Notre Dame, Indiana, provides the opportunity to teach, serve, and conduct research in the area of Speech Language Pathology. She currently teaches undergraduate and graduate speech-language pathology courses in the areas of speech and language development, assessment, and intervention, and provides clinical practicum supervision to graduate students.

1 Introduction

Chapter Overview

Chapter 1, "Introduction," serves as a foundation of understanding and the outlining of speech-language pathology practice and education requirements in the USA. Additionally, the chapter outlines the scope of practice and the process of speech-language pathology in various settings including, schools, private practice, healthcare, and early intervention. Information specific to the extensive and comprehensive roles and responsibilities of the speech-language pathologist is covered in the chapter, serving as a review for current practitioners and content building for leaders in education, including superintendents, human resource personnel, and district and building level administrators. Additionally, this chapter discusses the rationale for this study. Information on the current growing concerns about the poor retention of speech and language pathologists in schools is discussed; the growing need for speech and language services for children and students is grounded; and the increasing job requirements for speech and language pathologists in public schools are outlined.

***

Exploration and investigation of job satisfaction can be an important area of study in many professions, particularly when considering ways to recruit and retain highly qualified and effective employees. Finding career and job fulfillment is a goal for most people. Several questions emerge from this identified goal, this desire to find fulfillment and reward in the work we do. Do we enjoy the work we do each day? How do we find and maintain reward, satisfaction, and fulfillment within the broad and narrow scopes of our role, practice, or responsibilities? What factors impact the satisfaction we experience within the parameters of a job and a career path? As individuals, we may ask these questions from a place of personal growth and development or a desire to find the satisfaction within the scope of a current job position held or a wider and more long-term career plan. As leaders, we may approach these questions with a goal of enhancing recruitment efforts and maximizing retention potential.

Employers often strive to find ways to support this overall goal of individual employees and collective employee groups to find authentic job satisfaction. Employers may find benefit in understanding the roles, responsibilities, and needs of specific employee groups. The research study development, implementation, and results found within this book specifically focus on speech-language pathologists within a school environment. As a foundation for the research study discussion, a consideration of the way mindset has the potential to play a role in how an individual may view a current job or the facets of the job is valuable. Consideration of mindset is worth exploration in relation to perspectives, goals, and growth as it relates to an individual's job satisfaction.

Mindset

Let's begin with the exploration of research linked to mindset as a way to begin framing a component of the basis of this research study related to facet-based perceptions. Young people often develop a fixed or growth mindset beginning at an early age through interactions with parents, teachers, mentors, or other influential figures (Dweck, 2006). A fixed mindset is a focus on proving oneself in education, career, and personal relationships; at its root is the belief that each person has a certain personality type, level of intelligence, and moral character. Counter to the fixed mindset, the growth mindset identifies the basic qualities of intelligence, personality type, and moral character as a starting point from which to change, grow, and strive toward goals (Dweck, 2006). These opposing mindset perspectives have the potential to frame our approach to individual tasks, roles within our current job, willingness to take risks, attitude toward mistakes, and ability to personally and professional grow and develop. As leaders it may be beneficial to identify the values, beliefs, and work environment, specifically considering whether fixed or growth mindset is the basis for evaluation, mentoring, and completion of job duties. The research facets examined in the outlined study may offer a relevant opportunity to consider how mindset may factor into the work environment, with the potential to promote personal and professional growth, or alternatively inhibit creativity and optimal work performance.

Dweck (2006) suggested that humans have an innate love of learning. Yet, a person's motivation and mindset develop continually, changing with life's exposures, experiences, and opportunities to learn. Career opportunities and job facets are linked to these various exposures, ongoing experiences, and distinct learning opportunities that may shape an individual's motivation and mindset. Indeed, researchers may consider intrinsic and extrinsic motivation when studying the relationships between job satisfaction and various facets of a specific job. Both intrinsic drive and extrinsic motivation determine how individual interests, goals, and career path choices feed the innate human need for autonomy, self-determination, and connectedness (Pink, 2009).

It may prove valuable in studying job satisfaction to identify the ways growth mindset may offer opportunities to strive and grow based on flexibility, adaptability, and willingness to succeed and learn in the midst of perceived failure. Excitement and growth have the potential to offer opportunities for positive perceptions linked to needed flexibility and adaptability within a career path or specific job situation. Indeed, human nature drives an innate curiosity and need for self-direction. Because individuals are driven to find a path resulting in improvement of their life, having autonomy to make individual choices improves overall well-being (Pink, 2009). In considering the continuous evolving speech-language pathology roles and responsibilities, as well as the breadth and depth of the speech-language pathology field, there is an ongoing need for flexibility, adaptation, and willingness to grow, grounded in the study, research, and understanding of the implications of a growth mindset.

Public schools in Indiana struggle to recruit and retain speech-language pathologists. High caseload numbers, increased workload, and growing responsibilities are contributing to speech-language pathologist stress and burnout (Coordinating Committee of the Vice President for Speech-Language Pathology Practice, 2009). Because of diverse work environments and job aspects, speech-language pathologists respond to various intrinsic and extrinsic motivators, which influence their career trajectory, work setting choices, and retention of speech-language pathologists at various stages of their career paths. Speech and language skills correlate closely to academic success and achievement, highlighting the importance of the speech-language pathologist's role in the educational environment. Yet, the demands on speech-language pathologists continue to increase without solutions for preventing burnout and promoting job satisfaction. Woltmann and Camron (2009) stated that the speech-language pathologist shortages in school-based settings, primarily resulting from large caseloads and increased paperwork requirements, can result in underserved students in need of speech and language evaluation and intervention. It is important to consider the impact of this shortage of speech-language pathologists on needed student support, as well as the systemic educational need for speech and language expertise on school teams. Public school-based speech-language pathologists have experienced an increased need for flexibility, adaptation, management of expanding job responsibilities, and role adjustments as the field continues to evolve and the scope of practice grows. School district leaders face the challenge of recruiting and retaining public school-based speech-language pathologists in a competitive market. The field has evolved to include working with a diverse population and addressing a multitude of disorders and impairments in a variety of settings. Multiple opportunities and career decisions exist, including the selection of audiology or speech-language pathology, preferred client population and work setting, and desired employment facility (Leonard, Plexico, Plumb, & Sandage, 2016).

The field of speech-language pathology encompasses a comprehensive landscape of assessment and intervention, with a primary focus on supporting effective and functional communication. This monograph aims to explore the job satisfaction of school-based speech-language pathologists in the USA, through investigation of a focused, quantitative research study conducted in schools in Indiana and the accompanying analysis and synthesis of the associated research evidence. This monograph serves to offer insights in terms of how educational administration and speech-language pathologists can work collaboratively to better understand and find solutions to the needs for increased job satisfaction of the speech-language pathologists practicing in a field where demand now exceeds supply (Bureau of Labor Statistics, 2019).

Few researchers have focused specifically on identifying how speech-language pathologists determine their career paths and job choices. Additionally, based on a review of the literature, researchers have not specifically focused investigation on job satisfaction in relation to specific job facets in the field of speech-language pathology. Few researchers have focused on public school-based speech-language pathologists' job satisfaction, specifically studying facet-based job satisfaction. Limited facet-based job satisfaction data specific to Indiana speech-language pathologists have been collected based on literature review prior to this study. A detailed understanding of speech-language pathologists' initial career decisions, the reasons for their subsequent employment choices, and the facets with the strongest correlation to job satisfaction can serve to inform employers about important recruitment, job satisfaction, and retention information to consider when developing and implementing recruitment and retention strategic plans.

Additional helpful research may include identifying the point when speech-language pathology students determine the path to follow and whether perceived facets of job satisfaction affect employee retention when new graduates transition into professional practice. Miller and Ciocci (2013) stated that new college students define academic focus areas, career, and clinical interests based on preferences, experiential opportunities, and job characteristics. The national need for speech-language pathologists in public schools, necessary for meeting the needs of eligible students, warrants research that may help increase job satisfaction, diminish burnout, and promote consistency and retention.

It may also be beneficial to explore career paths and preferences specific to the field of speech-language pathology. Although researchers have not extensively studied career path preferences of speech-language pathology students, I have gained insight into the decision-making process from studies involving medical students. Several factors may influence a student's choice of medical specialty, including sociodemographic factors, individual characteristics, and environmental considerations (Nieman, Holbert, & Bremer, 1986). Additional primary factors include clinical experiences, student attitudes toward career opportunities, exposure to a specific employment environment, and the academic institution's focus on research and clinical practice (Brooks, 1991). In addition to studies of medical students, general vocational theory is relevant to recruitment, hiring, and retention of speech-language pathologists in public-school settings.

We must also consider the overall structure, health, and vitality of an organization as a component of potential impact related to recruitment, retention, and the job satisfaction variable. Kramer, Brewer, and Maquire (2011) investigated the impact of healthy work settings on new graduates' transitions into the professional practice within the field of nursing. Although the study encompasses only the field of nursing, it provides considerations for speech-language pathologists transitioning from academic training and preparation programs to professional clinical practice. In the field of nursing, the physical, social, and interaction aspects of the environment, as well as organizational structures and the values and actions of people, affect the transition from the academic setting to professional practice (Pearson et al., 2007). In studying the research, it seems the most effective way to master a new professional role is to undertake cooperative tasks with people in the work environment. In the field of speech-language pathology, these opportunities exist within the practicum clinical experiences, research opportunities, and clinical fellowship year experiences embedded to varying degrees within undergraduate, graduate, and postgraduate programs and professional requirements.

Kramer and Schmalenberg (2002) described healthy work environments in the field of nursing as a system that involves interrelated components of people, organizational structures, and practices that allow nurses to provide quality patient care. Nursing graduates transitioning from academia to professional practice demonstrate high expectations for their first clinical professional practice work environment (Kramer et al., 2011). The new graduates expect a healthy work environment based on people, organizational structures, and practices to support high quality care, resulting in job satisfaction (Lacey et al., 2011). Kramer et al. (2011) suggested that a healthy work environment needs a foundation of strong leadership with collaboration to promote increased retention and productivity of nursing graduates transitioning into clinical practice. A need exists for similar studies of transitioning and veteran speech-language pathologists; however, perhaps we can gain relevant insight into expectations of new speech-language pathology graduates related to organizational structure and healthy work environment. As educational leaders, how might we support this transition of recent graduates from coursework and practicum into the professional realm of independent practice?

Facet-Based Research

The details of this quantitative study conducted in schools in Indiana, USA, included in the following chapters, will provide a foundation for important ongoing considerations and discussions surrounding job satisfaction, with a link to recruitment and retention of speech-language pathologists in school-based settings. The study offers an in-depth investigation of the relationships between five identified job facets of the school-based speech-language pathologist's job, and general job satisfaction as identified, organized, and measured by the Job Descriptive Index (JDI; Bowling Green State University, 2009a) and the Job in General Scale (JIG; Bowling Green State University, 2009b). Included is an investigation of the effects of people, work, pay, opportunities for promotion, and supervision on general job satisfaction, as measured by quantitative survey data collected from speech-language pathologists, licensed and employed by public-school districts and cooperatives within Indiana.

The information obtained during this research investigation and subsequent analysis will serve to inform educational leaders, speech-language pathology students, early career and experienced speech-language pathology clinicians, and research scholars of the impact of individual and specific job facets on general job satisfaction with a research focus on speech-language pathologists in the school-based setting. The study offers a foundation that can serve as a platform for understanding the field of speech-language pathology, as well as provide a springboard for school leaders to develop and implement stronger, more comprehensive recruiting and retention plans to support, recognize, value, and energize school-based speech-language pathologists. As school leaders, whether you are a superintendent, a human resource administrator, a district or building level administrator, a curriculum director, a school-based speech-language pathologist, another school-based leader, or a researcher responsible for working to build and contribute to high quality, effective learning opportunities for students, the following chapters provide information about the current growing concerns of the challenges of recruitment and retention of school-based speech-language pathologists; the growing need for speech and language services for students; and the increasing job roles and responsibilities of current and future speech-language pathologists in schools. Additionally, this study's investigation of school-based speech-language pathologists' perceptions of specified job facets, combined with the understanding of mindset, vocational theory, and organizational culture, offers an opportunity for educational leaders and speech-language pathologists to look at ways to effectively address shortages, continue supporting evidence-based practice, and develop professional communities built upon shared leadership with a primary goal of providing students with the system of support needed for educational success. Continued knowledge acquisition and participation in ongoing discussions related to recruitment and retention is important for speech-language pathologists and the students who are served by these important team members.

Definition of Terms

In continuing the introduction to the speech-language pathology field and the practice of speech-language pathologists, as well as the focused research study found within this monograph, definitions for several related terms are outlined, providing a foundation for the research and discussion included in this monograph. The list of terms and definitions is not all-inclusive when considering all aspects and factors related to the field; however, a basis of knowledge specific to the field of speech-language pathology and the study of job satisfaction related to this study are relevant and important prior to in-depth investigation of the study and results included in the following chapters.

> *American Speech-Language-Hearing Association (ASHA)* is the nationally recognized professional, research, and credentialing body for the speech-language pathology field, with the mission and vision of communication as a human right for all (ASHA, 1997–2020).
> *Caseload* is the direct and/or indirect services provided to students identified as needing speech and/or language services as evidenced by Individual Education Plan (IEP) eligibility and implementation within the educational setting. Caseload can be summarized as a portion of the speech-language pathologist's workload, specifically the number of students receiving services from a speech-language pathologist (ASHA, 2002).

Job Descriptive Index (JDI) is a facet-based job satisfaction measure used to determine employee satisfaction with his or her job. The five facets include coworkers, work, pay, promotion, and supervision (Bowling Green State University, 2009a).

Job in General Scale (JIG) is a scale used to measure global job satisfaction (Bowling Green State University, 2009b).

Job satisfaction, as defined by Smith, Kendall, and Hulin (1969), is feelings experienced by an individual in relation to a specific job.

Speech-language pathologists are professionals who work to prevent, evaluate, diagnose, and remediate communication deficits and disorders in multiple areas, including speech, language, social, communicative cognition, and child and adult dysphagia (ASHA, 1997–2020).

Workload encompasses various activities supported by school-based speech-language pathologists, including collaboration, paperwork, and additional assigned duties, including but not limited to direct speech and language service delivery (ASHA, 2002).

Speech-Language Pathology Overview

In order to investigate the job satisfaction of speech-language pathologists practicing in school settings, we must first build knowledge of the field of speech-language pathology. The field of speech-language pathology has an evolving and complex scope of practice, including roles and responsibilities spanning education, medical, and research environments. Understanding the breadth, depth, and complex nature of speech-language pathology practice, including school-based speech-language pathology practice, may offer an important platform for developing recruitment and retention plans with a goal of increased and sustained job satisfaction.

Speech-language pathologists provide specialized speech and language assessment and intervention focused on speech and language acquisition, development, and rehabilitation in a variety of settings, including long-term care, medical-based facilities, private practice, clinical settings, and schools. Many identify speech-language pathologists almost exclusively with the correction of inaccurately articulated speech sounds or improving overall speech clarity. Although speech sound disorders, including articulation disorders, phonological disorders, and apraxia of speech, are an important focus in the field, it is also important to understand the comprehensive effective and functional communication focus of assessment and intervention, including the language aspects of communication. Language is composed of oral and written expression, listening and reading comprehension, and social pragmatics. A combination of the speech and language components of communication are an important foundation for literacy development, necessary for reading and writing. Language is an important component of all academic learning and social interactions. This is an important consideration when identifying the role of the speech-language pathologist participating on educational diagnostic and intervention teams, as well as Multi-tiered Systems of Support (MTSS) and Response to Intervention (RTI) teams. Speech-language pathologists have a primary role as an interventionist; therefore, inclusion of these professionals on school-based intervention teams with a goal of speech, language, and literacy support is a valuable resource for student success.

Speech-Language Pathologist Credentialing

In order to begin the additional exploration of this research study, it is also beneficial to understand the history of the credentialing entity and process. The American Speech-Language-Hearing Association (ASHA), founded in 1925, is the nationally recognized professional credentialing body for the speech-language pathology field. ASHA advocates for communication as a human right for all people (ASHA, 1997–2020). ASHA's mission focuses on assurance of accessible, effective communication for all individuals (ASHA, 1997–2020). ASHA's leaders strive to promote this mission by supporting practicing clinicians through research investigations and findings, accountability for high standards, promotion of professional excellence, and ongoing advocacy in the field of speech-language pathology. ASHA provides ongoing support to credentialed speech-language pathologists through opportunities for maintaining current knowledge of evidence-based practices, legal requirements, and continued professional development to meet the growing needs and changing roles and responsibilities within the field.

Indeed, not all speech-language pathologists obtain and maintain the ASHA Certificate of Clinical Competence in Speech-Language Pathology, or CCC-SLP; however, speech-language pathologists holding the distinct ASHA Certificate of Clinical Competence status have completed a master's and/or doctoral degree or post-baccalaureate degree recognized by ASHA; completed a postgraduate experience, typically called the Clinical Fellowship Year (CFY); and passed the required national examination (ASHA, 2016a). Although the Certificate of Clinical Competence is not required for practice in all settings, it provides an assurance of the achievement of rigorous academic and professional standards with an ongoing requirement for a continuous commitment to ongoing professional development and growth (ASHA, 1997–2020).

As the breadth and depth of speech-language pathology practice continues to grow, resulting in the redefinition of the speech-language pathologist's roles and responsibilities, continued professional growth and research of evidence-based practice must continue. It is imperative to consider the current and growing content, theory, and clinical application within the field. The outlined scope of practice landscape provides a foundation for the focused research study investigation of speech-language pathologist job satisfaction, specifically focused on the school-based speech-language pathologist.

Scope of Practice

Speech-language pathologists have a broad and growing scope of practice encompassing the following professional domains:

- advocating;
- clinical supervision;
- education;
- administrative tasks; and
- leadership in the field.

(ASHA, 2016b)

Additionally, speech-language pathology practice also includes the following research and service delivery domains:

- working collaboratively;
- providing counseling;
- prevention and overall wellness;
- screening;
- diagnostics;
- intervention;
- technology;
- instrumentation; and
- populations and systemic roles.

(ASHA, 2016b)

Investigation of the scope of practice, which has been outlined, highlights the varied and comprehensive nature of the field of speech-language pathology. As a result of the aging baby-boomer population, as well as advancements in medical intervention for preterm babies, an increase in health conditions resulting in speech and/or language impairments is expected, resulting in projected speech-language pathology employment growth equal to 27% between 2018 and 2028 (Bureau of Labor Statistics, 2019). The demand will likely exceed the supply, leaving employers with unmet needs for highly qualified, licensed, and credentialed speech-language pathologists, particularly in school-based settings. This shortage will impact the ability to meet the needs of patients, clients, and students. Public-school recruiters will need to act competitively in a job market with long-term care, medical-based facilities, private practice, and other clinical practice employment opportunities to recruit and retain speech-language pathologists to continue to meet the growing demand.

The high demand, combined with the potentially inadequate supply of graduating speech-language pathologists with a desire to work in the school setting, will likely result in additional recruiting, hiring, and retention challenges for school districts and special education cooperatives. To compete in a stretched market, schools need to continue to develop and strengthen the understanding of the relationships among specific job facets and job satisfaction. By examining the significance of specifically identified job facets impacting job satisfaction, contributions can be made to the fields of speech-language pathology and education. The limited existing research specific to facet-based job satisfaction and the need for focused recruitment and retention efforts, in order to meet the speech and language needs of students, make this study significant and relevant for current educational leaders. This research study and accompanying analysis provide information regarding the specific relationship of five specific job facets to job satisfaction. The research results provide information to build an understanding of general job satisfaction and the impact of individual job facets on the overall job satisfaction of school-based speech-language pathologists, leading to valuable and essential recruitment and retention discussions.

Schools face an increasing and ongoing shortage of school-based speech-language pathologists. It is important to consider the negative impact the shortage of speech-language pathologists may have on the learning and success of students in need of speech and language assessment and intervention, which is directly linked to student academic and life success. Functional and effective communication is an essential aspect in the lives of each and every person on a daily basis. Speech-language pathologists have the ability to play a key role in supporting individuals who experience challenges in the domains of communication. Ensuring learners have the opportunity to access these speech and language assessment and intervention services when needed is a charge that must be taken seriously. Ensuring that authentic and solution-based discussions specific to the job satisfaction of school-based speech-language pathologists are included at administrative levels is an important first step in beginning to solve current recruitment and retention challenges. Additionally, providing a forward-thinking foundation for promoting fulfilling and rewarding job opportunities to speech-language pathologists within school-based settings can energize the collaborative work of professional school communities.

Bibliography

American Speech-Language-Hearing Association. (1997–2020). *About the American Speech-Language-Hearing Association (ASHA)*. Retrieved from www.asha.org

American Speech-Language-Hearing Association. (2002). *A workload analysis approach for establishing speech-language caseload standards in schools: Technical report* [Position statement]. Retrieved from www.asha.org/policy

American Speech-Language-Hearing Association. (2016a). *Scope of practice in speech-language pathology* [Scope of Practice]. Retrieved from www.asha.org/policy/

American Speech-Language-Hearing Association. (2016b). *2016 schools survey report: SLP caseload characteristics*. Retrieved from www.asha.org/research/memberdata/schoolssurvey/

Bowling Green State University. (2009a). *The Job Descriptive Index 2009 revision*. Retrieved from www.bgsu.edu/arts-and-sciences/psychology/services/job-descriptive-index.html

Bowling Green State University. (2009b). *The Job in General scale*. Retrieved from www.bgsu.edu/arts-and-sciences/psychology/services/job-descriptive-index.html

Brooks, C. H. (1991). The influence of medical school clinical experiences on career preferences: A multidimensional perspective. *Social Science & Medicine, 32*(3), 327–332.

Bureau of Labor Statistics, U.S. Department of Labor. (2019). *Occupational outlook handbook, speech-language pathologists, on the Internet*. Retrieved from www.bls.gov/ooh/healthcare/speech-language-pathologists.htm

Coordinating Committee of the Vice President for Speech-Language Pathology Practice. (2009). Role ambiguity and speech-language pathology. *ASHA Leader, 14*(16), 12–15.

Dweck, C. (2006). *Mindset: The new psychology of success*. New York, NY: Ballantine Books.

Kramer, M., Brewer, B. B., & Maquire, P. (2011). Impact of healthy work environments on new graduate nurses' environmental reality shock. *Western Journal of Nursing Research, 35*(3), 348–383.

Kramer, M., & Schmalenberg, C. (2002). Staff nurses identify essentials of magnetism. In M. McClure & A. S. Hinshaw (Eds.), *Magnet hospitals revised: Attraction and retention of professional nurses*. Silver Spring, MD: American Nurses Association.

Lacey, S. R., Teasley, S., Cox, K. S., Olney, A., Kramer, M., & Schmalenberg, C. (2011). Development and testing of an organizational job satisfaction tool: Increasing precision for strategic improvements. *Journal of Nursing Administration, 41*, 15–22.

Leonard, M. V., Plexico, L. W., Plumb, A. M., & Sandage, M. J. (2016). Emerging practice preference of speech-language pathology students. *Contemporary Issues in Communication Science and Disorder, 43*, 285–298.

Miller, S. M., & Ciocci, S. R. (2013). Agents of change: Undergraduate students' attitudes following observations of speech-language pathology service deliver. *Journal of Allied Health, 42*(3), 141–146.

Nieman, L. Z., Holbert, D., & Bremer, C. C. (1986). Career preferences and decision-making habits of first-year medical students. *Academic Medicine, 61*(8), 644–653.

Pearson, A., Laschinger, B. N., Porritt, K., Jordan, Z., Tucker, D., & Long, L. (2007). Comprehensive systematic review of evidence on developing and sustaining nursing leadership that fosters a healthy work environment in healthcare. *International Journal of Evidence Based Healthcare, 5,* 208–253.

Pink, D. (2009). *Drive: The surprising truth about what motivates us.* New York, NY: Riverhead Books.

Smith, P. C., Kendall, L. M., & Hulin, C. L. (1969). *The measurement of satisfaction in work and retirement.* Chicago, IL: Rand McNally.

Woltmann, J., & Camron, S. C. (2009). Use of workload analysis for caseload establishment in the recruitment and retention of school-based speech language pathologists. *Journal of Disability Policy Studies, 20*(3), 178–183.

2 Understanding Speech-Language Pathology Practice in the Educational Setting

Chapter Overview

Chapter 2, "Understanding Speech-Language Pathology Practice in the Educational Setting," outlines the vast and diverse nature of the speech-language pathologist's roles and responsibilities in the educational setting. Although many are aware of the general practice of the school-based speech-language pathologist, few understand the complexities and domains impacted by the role of the speech-language pathologist. In order to examine the job satisfaction of school-based speech-language pathologists, it is important to understand and build awareness of the scope and landscape of clinical practice in the educational setting. This chapter highlights the growth of the breadth and depth of practice and outlines the discussion of a caseload and workload approach that will assist school administration in collaborating with individual school-based speech-language pathologists as well as the collective group. This chapter also provides insight into the importance of considering the collaborative power built from a mutual understanding and respect of the fields of education and speech-language pathology to support students.

***

Exploration and explanation of the roles and responsibilities of speech-language pathologists, specifically school-based clinical practice, is necessary before investigating the impact of specific job facets on general job satisfaction. School-based speech-language pathologists provide speech and language diagnostic and intervention services to support education across all school levels, including early childhood, primary, middle, and high school (ASHA, 2010). Additionally, in some cases, speech-language pathologists may continue to provide services in school-based young adult education programs, supporting additional functional and effective communication goals for vocational experiences, community involvement, and post-secondary opportunities.

Speech-language pathologists support receptive and expressive language skills and speech sound skills associated with student learning across all curricular domains, with a focus on language and literacy. The communication modalities of speech and language reach far beyond simply considering oral expression. Listening comprehension, reading comprehension, and written expression are important and necessary language domains for successful and meaningful academic and social experiences. The speech-language pathologist's roles and responsibilities extend beyond direct service delivery and include collaboration with parents and other educators, leadership at the building and district levels, supervision of Clinical Fellowship Year (CFY) speech-language pathologists, supervision of speech-language pathology support personnel, curriculum support, and collaboration with education colleagues. Each of these roles and responsibilities has the potential to positively impact the educational experience of individual students, as well as collective student progress linked to speech and language, supporting the meeting of academic standards and competencies.

ASHA (2014) identified the broad areas of speech-language pathology practice as education, research, and healthcare. The growth of the field's scope of practice has driven a redefinition and expansion of roles and responsibilities for practicing clinicians. The Coordinating Committee of the Vice President for Speech-Language Pathology Practice (2009) stated the most significant growth component is the increased collaboration and understanding of multidisciplinary team approaches to client care and intervention. School settings provide the opportunity for multidisciplinary team-based assessment and intervention to support students in all learning domains, with a comprehensive and whole-child approach to assessment and intervention, specific to learning outcomes. Paul and Norbury (2012) noted that students receiving language intervention during the Language for Learning period, which is the linguistic development during the adolescent years, often require transdisciplinary planning, which encompasses a team of specialists and teachers working together within and across disciplines to ensure an effective intervention plan. Identifying the importance of embracing a multidisciplinary team is important, but ensuring the speech-language pathologist is included on the team should be emphasized. Although the concept and practice of multidisciplinary team approaches is not novel or innovative within the scope of practice, it does require intentional effort and planning to achieve a successful implementation and outcome. The collaborative practice is a key factor in supporting students with the development, mastery, and generalization of communication skills, including speech and language, at all educational levels. Collaboration with teachers, parents, students, and other multidisciplinary team members is a growing aspect of the speech-language pathologist's role. Recognition and comprehensive understanding of the value of this role is continuing to evolve. It is important to note the importance of collaboration in promoting generalization of speech and language skills into daily life routines, learning activities, and various situations. Although mastery of skills is important, generalization is the overarching goal of speech and language intervention. If the primary goal is effective and functional communication within a student's natural contexts and environments, we must identify the need for collaborative discussion, planning, and implementation, combined with inclusion of all relevant members on a student's educational team. Without a solid foundational understanding of the resources the speech-language pathologist can offer as a member of the educational team, valuable opportunities for important collaboration may be unintentionally missed.

Speech-language pathology practice encompasses a much larger landscape than the traditional pull-out intervention approaches. It is important to note that assessment and intervention should always be based on individual student needs and supportive practices for increased and improved effective and functional communication. The focus on functional communication emphasizes the importance of connecting speech and language intervention to curriculum standards and contextualized language. The individualized planning and implementation focused on generalization of effective and functional communication skills may include a combination of service delivery approaches and models. Speech and language assessment and intervention are not uniform in nature, but instead provide a framework built upon theoretical constructs and research-based practices to provide individualized student support based on strengths and needs. The support builds upon strengths while targeting areas of deficit to promote a goal of generalized communication skills. This essential collaborative speech-language pathologist role provides an opportunity to support student communication growth across the school curriculum and contexts, both in the school academic and social environments. Although progress within a specific intervention session should be celebrated, the goal of generalization across contexts and environments builds a sustainable and functional communication system: the true goal of a speech-language pathologist's work.

While the need has increased for a better understanding of the speech-language pathologist's specific roles and responsibilities in recent decades, it is important to consider how the client population has also grown in cultural and linguistic diversity. These two factors have converged, offering the potential need for a role redefinition and expansion. Stewart and Gonzalez (2002) completed a national study to investigate how master's-level speech-language pathology programs are preparing professionals for the need to serve a more diverse population. They measured how programs attract, retain, and achieve graduation with speech-language pathology students from diverse backgrounds. ASHA (1998) supported the efforts of master's-level preparation programs to ensure appropriate preparation to provide assessment and intervention with a culturally and linguistically diverse client population and provide necessary training for future speech-language pathologists. It is essential to ensure that continued focus on evidence-based practice with consideration of cultural and linguistic diversity is at the center of speech-language pathology practice. Each assessment and intervention plan must be individualized to recognize strengths and meet the comprehensive needs of the individual student and family, while ensuring an emphasis on cultural competency. Working collaboratively as a cohesive educational team provides a platform to have discussions and build systems that support the learning of all students based on diverse individual strengths and needs.

The development and implementation of tiered interventions offers support for a systemic approach to research-based instruction with embedded opportunities for student support, based on data-driven decisions. Providing optimal educational opportunities for all students points to the continued importance of research-based Tier 1 intervention. In order to determine if a student has a speech or language impairment, there must be access to appropriate Tier 1 general education research-based instruction. Speech-language pathologists can offer valuable language and literacy information based on evidence-based practices for all intervention tiers, including Tier 2 and Tier 3, using data to support appropriate additional supports, including small group instruction, increased frequency or intensity of interventions, or individualized instruction. Unfortunately, speech-language pathologists are sometimes not invited into these discussions. Often, it is not an intentional exclusion, but rather a lack of understanding of the link of the speech-language pathologist's scope of practice to the language expression and comprehension necessary for academic success. Speech-language pathologists have the potential to offer language and literacy strategies for all students. Given the role of prevention, providing ways to support all students with speech, language, and literacy development could serve to prevent the need of referral for special education assessment, and potentially future intervention for some students. Consider the contribution of the speech-language pathologist as a resource for phonemic awareness, written expression, vocabulary knowledge, and reading comprehension. These skills are linked significantly to the academic success of students in all subjects and ultimately the effective and functional communication system that is essential for life success, both socially and academically. Teachers and speech-language pathologists can work together collaboratively as a unified team to build highly effective systems for educating each and every student using collective knowledge, experience, and researched interventions.

Educational Leaders

Educational leaders are tasked with continuously developing, implementing, and improving systems, while utilizing and supporting staff effectively. Leaders have the opportunity to ensure speech-language pathologists are part of the development, planning, and implementation efforts at the school and district levels. The role of the speech-language pathologist on each individual team may need to be defined to ensure meaningful and productive participation, but the value of initiating these discussions is worth exploring in order to build a strong foundation for positive systemic impact. Invitations to participate as members of school improvement teams, tiered intervention system development and implementation, grade level data analysis, reading intervention and instruction professional development, and literacy curriculum professional development and implementation may enhance collegial relationships and build collaborative practice opportunities to provide stronger support for student success. Core knowledge of language and literacy contributes to the overall goals of the school community. Comprehensive understanding of the identified methods and practices for developing and solidifying these skills, within the context of educational curriculum and functional communication by all team members, supports the generalization of learned skills beyond isolated educational events or contexts to real-life contextualized experiences.

Caseload and Workload

As mentioned previously, speech-language pathologists have varied employment opportunities. Some professionals may choose a work setting based strictly on a preference for serving a specific age group (Leonard, Plexico, Plumb, & Sandage, 2016). Edgar and Rosa-Lugo (2007) stated that although more speech-language pathologists are employed by public schools than ever before, the shortage in the school-based setting has reached critical levels in many cases. Half of all employed US speech-language pathologists are employed in school settings (Ghazzawi, 2006). Excessive paperwork and large caseloads are the primary identified reasons for the reported speech-language pathologist shortage (ASHA, 2014). ASHA (2004) reported that school-based speech-language pathologists provide support services to over two million students in first through twelfth grades. It is important to note this data does not include the important Pre-K early intervention years or the post-secondary young adult program services.

Continuing the discussion of caseload and workload is important in the understanding of school-based speech-language pathology clinical practice. Field specific terminology may increase the challenge of discussing and understanding the speech-language pathologist's role for those related to but not practicing as licensed and credentialed speech-language pathology clinicians in the education field. Although school administrators may not have detailed knowledge of the vast landscape of speech-language pathology practice, it will be beneficial to gain an understanding of important terminology used often within the field to promote and support robust, collaborative discussion. To study potential factors contributing to recruitment challenges, increased work stress, and high attrition rates, it is necessary to understand two terms: caseload and workload.

ASHA (2002) defined caseload as the direct and/or indirect services provided to students identified as needing speech and/or language services as evidenced by Individualized Education Plan (IEP) eligibility, development, and implementation. Caseload is a portion of the speech-language pathologist's workload proportional to the number of eligible students receiving services on the individual speech-language pathologist's caseload. Conversely, workload refers to the compilation of activities supported by school-based speech-language pathologists, including collaboration, paperwork, and additional assigned duties (ASHA, 2002). Workload extends beyond service delivery to all tasks related to supporting a single eligible student. Adding a single student to a caseload increases evaluation and service delivery responsibilities (Edgar & Rosa-Lugo, 2007). Thus, the addition of an individual student contributes to the caseload number, but also increases the overall workload. The amount of increase is based on each student's individual communication needs, the complexity of the case, and the level of support needed. Speech-language pathologists stated they spend 70% of their time supporting direct intervention activities and diagnostic evaluation (Zingeser, 2004). Limited time remains for engaging in effective collaboration, consultation, and other assigned duties encompassing workload aspects of practice. The lack of time to perform tasks, such as collaboration, that speech-language pathologists identify as important for teamwork, relationship building, and student success may contribute to feelings of inadequacy or ineffectiveness, resulting in decreased job satisfaction and ultimately a higher attrition rate. It is important to understand the distinction between caseload and workload to ensure an accurate picture of the speech-language pathologist's role within a school building and school system. Simply identifying caseload numbers provides a limited understanding of the speech-language pathologist's workload.

State and local regulations guide caseload size mandates and implementation. Although ASHA recommends a maximum caseload of 40 students, with a reduced caseload of 25 students for special populations, caseloads in many states exceed the maximum recommended numbers (Edgar & Rosa-Lugo, 2007). Blood, Thomas, Ridenour, Qualls, and Hammer (2002) stated speech-language pathologists responsible for higher caseloads experienced lower job satisfaction. The question arises, are the higher caseload numbers the true source of lower job satisfaction, or must we consider the overall workload resulting from higher caseloads? Would a workload model serve to offer increased clarity of the true underlying factors contributing to increased job satisfaction or, alternately, job dissatisfaction and burnout? These are questions we must consider in the study of speech-language pathology job satisfaction, particularly as we explore ways to support and improve effective school-based recruitment and retention practices.

The study included in this monograph was developed to study school-based speech-language pathologists practicing in Indiana, USA. As a result, it is important to outline caseload numbers relevant to this study when compared to the ASHA's recommended caseload numbers. Indiana significantly exceeds the maximum recommended caseload in school settings with a record-high average size of 75 students (ASHA, 2004). More children than ever need speech and language services, and more students in related disability categories need speech and language intervention as well (ASHA, 2002). Speech-language pathologists provide important speech and language services to students with primary and secondary speech and language eligibilities within school environments. Many related primary eligibility categories are often accompanied by a secondary speech or language impairment, impacting effective and functional communication in a single way or multitude of ways. As we consider the impact of workload, it should be considered that an increased workload may reduce time for collaboration among professionals and increases recruitment challenges, attrition rates, and job dissatisfaction. It is important to understand that while setting a caseload cap may seem a simple solution to the identified speech-language pathologist burden, careful consideration is recommended. Several additional challenges surface with the concept of implementing a caseload cap, including an increased demand for additional speech-language pathologists within a shortage area, caseload numbers based on identified students without consideration of the exclusion of tiered intervention involvement, a lack of consideration for workload as a component of caseload numbers, and the possibility of decreased autonomy with regards to eligibility and dismissal decisions.

Peters-Johnson (1998) found that 53% of school-based clinicians are responsible for a caseload between 40 and 69 students and spend an average of 21.5 hours each week serving students directly. The large caseloads and increased workloads identified in current literature make collaboration especially important. Collaborative service delivery models allow speech-language pathologists to meet students' needs while managing large caseloads, ultimately improving job satisfaction (Ehren & Ehren, 2001).

Additionally, generalization of skills may be positively impacted by a collaborative service delivery model to promote the extension of new skills across school and home environments or activities, such as recess, lunch, extracurricular activities, and the general education classroom. Extending the intervention across new environments, known as sequential modification, supports generalization of new skills in various contexts (Costello, 1983). An ongoing emphasis of individualized assessment and intervention will be found embedded across all chapters of this monograph. Pull-out, integrated, contextualized, and hybrid intervention models can all support various student needs; however, the educational team must assess and determine the most effective approach or combination of approaches for an individual child's communication needs. Dynamic assessment and ongoing progress monitoring with defined data collection and collaborative analysis can offer continuous information for ensuring intervention approaches for optimal student progress. Speech-language pathologists are unable, and should not attempt, to accomplish this in isolation. Parents, general and special education teachers, and other educational team members in a student's life should be involved in determining current progress and future goals to promote generalized effective and functional communication skills. In order to accomplish this goal, time for collaboration within the context of caseload and workload is a necessary consideration.

ASHA (2016) surveyed school-based speech-language pathologists and educational audiologists. Analysis of the data identified most providers (81%) used a caseload approach for caseload management, fewer (15%) utilized a workload approach, and only 4% used a combined approach. Based on the results of the survey, a typical caseload includes 43% of students with moderate impairments. In a survey of school-based clinicians, Katz, Maag, Fallon, Blenkarn, and Smith (2010) found that most surveyed participants (59.1%) reported caseloads to be unmanageable at a threshold of 55 students. Another 38.5% of participants reported caseloads to be unmanageable at 56–60, and approximately 20% reported caseloads to be unmanageable at 41–45 students. Considering caseload numbers in isolation provides only a snapshot instead of a comprehensive picture of the roles and responsibilities of the speech-language pathologist. Consider a student with an articulation error of /r/ that mildly impacts a student's speech production and a student who requires the use of an Augmentative and Alternative Communication device (AAC) for effective communication. Both students have individual needs that may require important speech and/or language intervention to improve effective and functional communication. Each individual student would add to the caseload numbers of a speech-language pathologist. However, it is likely the support needed by each of these students based on individualized strengths, needs, and plans to meet their needs would contribute in different ways to the overall workload. One must take into consideration the additional time needed to effectively support each student. In considering the use of an AAC device, it is important to account for the potential need for setup, teacher training, and parent education for use of the AAC communication system across multiple environments and contexts. Consider potential time needed to ensure the student is able to effectively generalize functional use of the AAC device in the general education setting. All of these factors must be included in the workload calculation. In exploring the needs of the student with the articulation error, establishing and stabilizing the correct production, maintaining the accurate production, and then generalizing across contexts are included in the plan. Time is needed to collaborate with the teacher to determine if the error is occurring in written expression, discuss ways to increase sound production and practice, and support generalization to conversational speech. In both cases, teacher, parent, and student involvement is an essential component of striving for optimal student success. Time for collaboration is a necessary consideration for implementation of these optimal plans for improving functional communication effectiveness.

Speech-language pathologists, like all educators, strive to effectively meet student needs to ensure optimal success; however, when faced with limited time for collaboration, problem-solving, and data analysis, work stress and burnout are potential outcomes that surface. It is ineffective and short-sighted to consider only caseload numbers when determining speech-language pathologist staffing needs, given that the accompanying workload is not defined by numbers alone. Caseload should be a factor in understanding the roles and responsibilities of the speech-language pathologist, but providing an opportunity for the speech-language pathologist to outline the workload gives way to initiating much-needed discussion and a more comprehensive understanding.

Supporting Students

In order to ensure that students receive the appropriate and necessary support for educational success, caseloads and workloads have increased as a result of the Education for All Handicapped Act of 1975 and 1986 and the Individuals with Disabilities Education Act of 1990, 1991, 1997, and 2004. These laws and regulations provide necessary protection of the rights of students with disabilities. Laws, mandates, and regulations such as these have increased the need for a specialized skill base; expanded involvement with reading, writing, and literacy; and affected professional collaboration and standard best practices (Coordinating Committee of the Vice President for Speech-Language Pathology Practice, 2009). Early special education laws encompassed assurances of a free and appropriate public education

(FAPE) within the least restrictive environment (LRE), with a provision of IEPs. The Individuals with Disabilities Education Act reauthorizations in 1997 and 2004 emphasized accountability for connections to educational results, requiring

- increased parent engagement and participation;
- identification of student strengths and parent concerns;
- student curriculum progress, specifically meeting academic standards;
- evidence-based and researched reading instruction;
- inclusion of general educators as part of the team, including development and implementation of the IEP;
- inclusion of students identified with a special education eligibility in district assessing and reporting; and
- quality professional practice standards for professionals providing services to students with identified special education needs.

(Paul & Norbury, 2012)

Additionally, the Every Student Succeeds Act (ESSA; 2015) once again increases the necessary and important accountability related to school success. The law offered funding for a Comprehensive Literacy Center, mandated only 1% of students be allowed to participate in alternate assessments, offered grants for literacy intervention, provided family engagement resources, and supported professional development for teachers working with children identified with disabilities. ESSA's mandates provide a continued platform for the emphasized importance of the role of speech-language pathologists as collaborative partners in literacy intervention for students with identified language impairments. Speech-language pathology practice is built upon a foundation of language and literacy development, family engagement practices, and professional learning opportunities as supported by ASHA's goal of providing accessible functional communication to all individuals as a human right. These components of speech-language pathology practice, combined with the increased focus on literacy as a pillar of ESSA, provide a strong platform to increase focus on the role of a speech-language pathologist as a team member on school-based literacy teams. Additionally, I might suggest considerations for ways to develop or enhance collaborative or team-teaching methodology, combining the knowledge and expertise of teachers and speech-language pathologists to enhance reading, writing, and literacy instruction. ESSA provides an opportunity to continue and enhance the discussions about the role of the speech-language pathologist in relationship to language and literacy. Additionally, the discussion has the potential to expand to determining and defining the team member role of the speech-language pathologist, specific to literacy development and instruction. Provision of autonomy for schools to determine and define these roles offers the flexibility and adaptability to build a solid system built on researched methods within systemic school structures and cultures, supporting individual district, school building, grade level, classroom, and individual student needs.

Regulations have caused additional challenges that require consideration, including

- increased lack of time for collaboration;
- lack of guidance information related to team-oriented and multidisciplinary service delivery;
- limited specific knowledge of related professionals' roles; and
- lack of team cohesiveness based on time needed to build trust and mutual respect, which is a barrier to an effective and optimal team approach.

(Coordinating Committee of the Vice President for Speech-Language Pathology Practice, 2009)

Alternatively, regulations have caused positive outcomes, including

- a multidisciplinary team-oriented service delivery model promoting diversified planning and implementation;
- specialization;
- support for intervention tasks spanning across professions to support students;
- horizontal substitution, providing valuable support for staff shortages;
- an increase in potential for a collaborative work environment; and
- team-oriented service delivery models and treatment approaches.

(Nancarrow & Borthwick, 2005)

The rewarding and challenging components associated with speech-language pathology practice are evident. In Chapter 3, the discussion will continue with investigation and exploration of theoretical constructs that will provide the foundation for the research study based on the exploration of facet-based job satisfaction. Evidence deeply embedded in theory offers continued insight into the motivations, goals, and rewards informing the basis for school-based speech-language pathology job satisfaction research.

Bibliography

American Speech-Language-Hearing Association. (1998). Students and professionals who speak English with accents and nonstandard dialects: Issues and recommendations. Position statement and technical report. *ASHA Supplement, 18*(40), 28–31.

American Speech-Language-Hearing Association. (2002). *A workload analysis approach for establishing speech-language caseload standards in schools: Technical report* [Position statement]. Retrieved from www.asha.org/policy

American Speech-Language-Hearing Association. (2004). Clinical supervisor's responsibilities. *ASHA Supplement, 24*, 36–38.

American Speech-Language-Hearing Association. (2010). *Roles and responsibilities of speech-language pathologists in schools* [Position statement]. Retrieved from www.asha.org/policy

American Speech-Language-Hearing Association. (2014). *Careers in speech-language pathology: Many careers, many rewards*. Retrieved from www.asha.org/Students/Speech-Language-Pathologists/#careers

American Speech-Language-Hearing Association. (2016). *2016 schools survey report: SLP caseload characteristics*. Retrieved from www.asha.org/research/memberdata/schoolssurvey/

Blood, G. W., Thomas, E. A., Ridenour, J. S., Qualls, C. D., & Hammer, C. S. (2002). Job stress in speech-language pathologists working in rural, suburban, and urban schools: Social support and frequency of interactions. *Contemporary Issues in Communication Science and Disorders, 29*(2), 132–140.

Coordinating Committee of the Vice President for Speech-Language Pathology Practice. (2009). Role ambiguity and speech-language pathology. *ASHA Leader, 14*(16), 12–15.

Costello, J. (1983). Generalization across settings: Language intervention with children. In J. Miller, D. Yoder, & R. Schiefelbusch (Eds.), *Contemporary issues in language intervention*. Rockville, MD: American Speech-Language-Hearing Association.

Edgar, D. L., & Rosa-Lugo, L. I. (2007). The critical shortage of speech-language pathologists in the public school setting: Features of the work environment that affect recruitment and retention. *Language, Speech, and Hearing Sciences in Schools, 38*, 31–46.

Ehren, B. J., & Ehren, T. C. (2001). New or expanded literacy roles for speech-language pathologists: Making it happen in the schools. *Seminars in Speech and Language, 22*(3), 234–243.

Every Student Succeeds Act. (2015). Pub. L. No. 114–95. USC.

Ghazzawi, G. (2006). *2006 schools survey: Special report: Caseload trends*. Rockville, MD: American Speech-Language-Hearing Association.

Katz, L. A., Maag, A., Fallon, K. A., Blenkarn, K., & Smith, M. K. (2010). What makes a caseload (un)manageable? School-based speech-language pathologists speak. *Language, Speech, and Hearing Services in Schools, 41*, 139–151.

Leonard, M. V., Plexico, L. W., Plumb, A. M., & Sandage, M. J. (2016). Emerging practice preference of speech-language pathology students. *Contemporary Issues in Communication Science and Disorder, 43*, 285–298.

Nancarrow, S. A., & Borthwick, A. M. (2005). Dynamic professional boundaries in the healthcare workforce. *Sociology of Health and Illness, 27*, 897–919.

Paul, R., & Norbury, C. (2012). *Language disorders from infancy through adolescence: Listening, speaking, reading, writing, and communicating* (4th ed.). St. Louis, MO: Elsevier Mosby.

Peters-Johnson, C. (1998). Action: School services. *Language, Speech, and Hearing Services in Schools, 29,* 120–126.

Stewart, R., & Gonzalez, L. (2002). Serving a diverse population: The role of speech-language pathology professional preparation programs. *Journal of Allied Health, 31*(4), 204–216.

Zingeser, L. (2004). Career and job satisfaction. *The ASHA Leader, 9,* 4–13.

3 Understanding Motivating Factors to Support Speech-Language Pathology Job Satisfaction

Chapter Overview

Chapter 3, "Understanding Motivating Factors to Support Speech-Language Pathology Job Satisfaction," outlines the theoretical framework that informed this job satisfaction research study by investigating and discussing expectancy theory of motivation; motivational theory of role modeling; and social cognitive theory. Consideration of the aspects related to the career and job decision-making process offers the framework for public-school districts in Indiana, USA, to develop and implement an effective recruitment plan and decrease the shortage of public school-based speech-language pathologists in Indiana. Additionally, attempting to understand the theoretical constructs related to the motivation of individuals to remain in school-based speech-language pathology positions may offer beneficial insight for retention strategies in Indiana and nationwide. This chapter aims to connect the foundation of theory to the research investigation necessary in later chapters for discussion of research to practice connections.

***

Three theoretical constructs have framed this research of job satisfaction, occupational stress and burnout, and speech-language pathologists' future vocational decisions. The theoretical constructs include the expectancy theory of motivation, motivational theory of role modeling, and social cognitive theory.

Expectancy Theory of Motivation

Consideration of the aspects related to the career and job decision-making process offer the framework for public-school districts in Indiana, USA, to develop and implement an effective recruitment plan and work to potentially decrease the shortage of public school-based speech-language pathologists in Indiana. Additionally, attempting to understand the motivation of individuals to pursue and remain in school-based speech-language pathology positions may offer beneficial insight for recruitment and retention strategies in Indiana, nationwide, and worldwide, particularly in regions experiencing speech-language pathologist shortages in school-based clinical practice.

When discussing the impact and development of job-related motivation, it is important to identify that motivation and job expectations may change in relation to employer management and the overall health of a work environment. An accurate understanding of this relationship may help speech-language pathologists to make informed employment and retention decisions that are relevant to individual job and long-term career path decision-making. Providing multiple and varied opportunities and efforts to support accurate perceptions and insights for work within the school environment is important in developing a solid basis of information for speech-language pathologist recruitment and retention. Without individual experiences within a specified environment, individuals often rely on opinions and perceptions of others. Reliance on the opinions and perceptions of others may not reflect an authentic experience. Without the opportunities for authentic experiences, individuals may not be effectively able to formulate accurate perceptions based on their own individual values and opinions. As we begin to consider the role of theoretical constructs in developing relevant research specific to job satisfaction, as well as enhance the breadth and depth of recruitment and retention discussions, we will begin our discussion with the expectancy theory of motivation.

Victor Vroom's (1964) expectancy theory of motivation emphasizes that employee performance is connected to contributing factors, including individual personality, skills and abilities, knowledge, and experience. It is important to consider these specific facets when discussing the relevant link to job and career satisfaction. Vroom suggested individuals can be motivated if they believe that their effort and job performance will provide a resulting positive relationship. Additionally, individuals are motivated by awards resulting from good performance. Rewards that fulfill an individual need supporting the need to work at a specific level, a contribution to employee performance and motivation is achieved.

Expectancy theory of motivation outlines three concepts: valence, expectancy, and instrumentality. The premise of Vroom's (1964) expectancy theory of motivation is that individuals will exert a level of effort to meet performance expectations if the effort will result in a positive outcome and avoidance of pain. The potential for misalignment of experiences, expectations, and personally desired outcomes may be a contributing factor to the shortage of speech-language pathologists in Indiana public-school settings.

Vroom's (1964) expectancy theory of motivation differs from content theories in that content theories include no individual motivational suggestions. Vroom offered motivational strategies, including

- change of the effort and performance expectations;
- performance related to reward expectations; and
- reward preferences.

(as cited in Lunenburg, 2011)

Based on the expectancy theory assumptions, three key elements emerge:

- *expectancy*, or individuals' different expectations and levels of confidence;
- *instrumentality*, or the perception of the individual related to the desired outcome; and
- *valence*, or the emotional connection to outcomes and the desire for intrinsic or extrinsic rewards.

(Parijat & Bagga, 2014)

In considering Vroom's expectancy theory of motivation, it may be important to note that both school and healthcare speech-language pathologists report job satisfaction, yet it is significantly higher among healthcare speech-language pathologists (Kalkhoff & Collins, 2012). Whitehouse, Hird, and Cocks (2007) suggested that lack of retention may arise from unmet career expectations if expectations do not match experiences upon entering the speech-language pathology workforce. Consider early career speech-language pathologists with expectations of a specific job experience. Smith, Du, and Bedwinek (2015) reported speech-language pathologists employed in Missouri demonstrated job satisfaction specifically related to employment benefits, supervision, colleagues, type of work, and student progress. If career expectations are not met, perhaps resulting from high caseloads, unreasonable workloads, lack of supervisor support, or lack of collaboration opportunities, specifically related to facets identified as important for student and client educational success and achievement, it is possible the result will negatively impact retention efforts.

Vroom (1964) indicated that individuals are motivated to choose happiness with a focus on minimizing dissatisfaction and discomfort. If considering situations with negative interactions or practicum experiences prior to career choice, the potential is present that a speech-language pathologist candidate may choose job settings they do not perceive to bring dissatisfaction or discomfort. This contributes to the consideration of investigating the impact of speech-language pathology students' interactions with professors, clinical supervisors, and clinical practicum experiences to determine the impact on future employment setting choices. Perhaps these preservice experiences impact recruitment efforts of future employers.

Vroom (1964) outlined three aspects of occupational decision-making, including *occupational preference*, *occupational choice*, and *attainment*:

- *Occupational preference* includes careers of the most interest to the individual at any point during the decision-making process when there are no barriers present. When exploring the reason individuals choose specific job positions and career paths, several facets, situations, and values may contribute to the decision. For example, some college students may choose the field of speech-language pathology because of an occupational preference. This may prove relevant if the individual has an awareness and specific knowledge of the necessary skill set and scope of work necessary to succeed as a practicing speech-language pathologist, as well as the academic and clinical requirements to reach this goal. Additionally, individuals choosing to pursue a career in the field of speech-language pathology may possess intrinsic motivation to help people acquire, develop, and effectively utilize communication for optimal interactions and communicative engagement. The motivation aligns with the overall mission of ASHA, supporting the connection of personal goals to the mission and vision of the credentialing body for the profession in the USA.
- *Occupational choice* is a selection process between possible occupational choices of interest. This selection process results in the individual becoming focused on a chosen path. Vroom suggested that participation in a training program or internship may support and indicate occupational choice. Students exploring the options of audiology compared to speech-language pathology may experience occupational choice when reaching a point of decision-making, which may result in a focus on a specific course of study. Supporting individual interests and preferences, combined with opportunities for career exploration, can allow individuals the ability to authentically explore potential career paths.
- *Attainment*, the final step in Vroom's model, is the result of the occupational choice and includes the occupation the individual chooses. Importantly, Matteson and Smith (1977) showed that occupational choice and attainment rarely differed when they examined students making choices of medical specialty.

Motivational Theory of Role Modeling

While it is important to acquire and develop the role of expectations related to motivational impact, it is also important to consider the impact of role model influence in conjunction with expectancy theory of motivation. Role models are individuals in a defined role who provide examples of the behavior linked to a specific role (Merton, 1957). Morgenroth, Ryan, and Peters (2015) identified role models as individuals who motivate individuals to act on new behaviors and encourage ambitious goal-setting.

Morgenroth et al. (2015) suggested a motivational theory of role modeling. The researchers used the expectancy-value motivation model to determine that role models in speech-language pathology may contribute to the decision-making and goal-setting of novice students of speech-language pathology and early career speech-language pathologists. Morgenroth et al. (2015) identified three defining functions of a role model: modeling behavior, providing an example of what is possible, and offering inspiration. Recurring and interwoven themes exist among all of these role model functions. Themes include providing examples of skill performance and goal achievement, providing examples of goal attainment, and demonstrating desirability of goals (Morgenroth et al., 2015). Schools and other employers need to consider the impact of role models in speech-language pathology when interacting with future clinicians during coursework, practicum experiences, and ongoing employment opportunities to promote job satisfaction resulting in positive recruitment and retention efforts. Consider the potential impact of a positive and supportive role model who provides opportunities for career path discernment, as well as supports an individual in realizing the maximum potential for reaching goals, while taking time to actively listen to a student or early career speech-language pathologist's goals and aspirations, and models a growth mindset approach to problem-solving and critical thinking in practice. It may be valuable to consider the impact of modeled behavior on students and colleagues interacting with us. Modeling flexibility, adaptability, and realistic but positive approaches has the potential to inspire, support, and motivate.

Social Cognitive Theory

In addition to researching Vroom's (1964) individual expectancy theory and the motivational theory of role modeling (Morgenroth et al., 2015), it is important to investigate research related to the impact of cognition on making decisions. In 1961 and 1963, Albert Bandura expanded the social learning theory. Bandura showed a direct relationship between perception and behavioral change. Bandura suggested that self-efficacy comes from personal accomplishments, experiences and opportunities, verbal persuasion, and physiology (Bandura, 1977).

Bandura expanded the theory, now called social cognitive theory, including the role of cognition in human behavior and the cognitive results of personal, behavioral, and environmental influences (Bandura, 1986). Bandura (2001) promoted the use of social cognitive theory for analyzing the influence of communication on human thoughts and actions. Social cognitive theory has the potential to help in our discussions related to career choices, motivation, and learning.

Social cognitive career theory clarifies the processes for developing educational and vocational interests, career choices, and associated performance (Lent, Brown, & Hackett, 1994). The theory encompasses the relationships between cognitive-person variables, individual behavior, and contexts that limit or enhance personal agency. Cognitive-person variables include gender, ethnicity, barriers, and support systems (Lent et al., 2002).

Lent et al. (2002) found career decision makers' perceived interests, values, and abilities to be significant factors in the career choice process. Relatively few participants mentioned social and family influences as a factor in career choice. Instead, direct and indirect work experiences, including performance feedback and modeling, were influential career choice factors. Lent et al. suggested career exploration, including job shadowing and internships, as a way for individuals making career choices to clarify interests, values, and abilities related to career fields and associated tasks, roles, and responsibilities. The researchers referred to career interests as individual likes, dislikes, and feelings of indifference related to career activities (Lent et al., 1994). Based on these findings, it is reasonable to explore the need for clearly defined and diverse job shadowing and practicum experiences to provide an avenue for the identification of true interests, values, and abilities in order to ensure informed employment setting choices for speech-language pathologists. It is also important to consider the specific points during career exploration, program completion, and breadth of experiences offered. While exposure to speech-language pathology areas of interest is valuable and important, we may also want to consider identifying and providing opportunities extending beyond specified areas of interest. Exploring this concept further, consider the speech-language pathology student exposed to opportunities in the medical setting resulting from areas of interest, but without opportunities within a school environment; it is possible a student may not be aware of opportunities for working in a school setting. Breadth and depth of opportunities at various points during career exploration may support decision-making based in a broader understanding of all the speech-language pathology career path possibilities.

Social cognitive career theory emphasizes the generation of identified goals to pursue and completion of necessary academic and professional career tasks that align with individual interests, self-efficacy, and expectations (Hung-Bin et al., 2010). Social cognitive career theory also states that specific variables, including supports and challenges, shape career choice (Rogers & Creed, 2011). Lent et al. (1994) outlined two related levels of social cognitive career theory based on varying environmental factors. In the first level, individuals exert personal control with self-efficacy, expectations, and goal-setting. The second level encompasses additional variables, including physical attributes, environmental factors, and experiences that shape and influence career interests and choices. It is important to note that the levels are related and contribute to influential shaping of career goals and decision-making.

Based on the social cognitive career theory premise, career inquiry and development depend on objective information combined with environmental perceptions (Lent, Brown, & Hackett, 2000). Individual interpretation of various goals and environmental factors may allow for personal control of career development and choice-making. Speech-language pathology employers can improve recruitment efforts by accounting for exposure to the career (Stone & Pellowski, 2016). We should consider and ensure that we don't underestimate the potential impact of positive opportunities, interactions, and engagement with various facets of speech-language pathology in the discernment and decision-making of students and early career speech-language pathologists. Byrne (2007) found that prior exposure to the field, either by receiving speech and/or interventions or knowing a speech-language pathologist, emerged as a significant influential factor in choosing the field for a career path.

Based on projected future speech and language assessment and intervention needs, public school-based speech-language pathologists will continue to be in high demand in the future. The demand for speech and language assessment and intervention in school-based settings will persist, evidenced by increasing caseloads, roles, and responsibilities, and continuously evolving job descriptions, discussed in the literature. Determining the relationships among specific job facets and job satisfaction grounded in a strong theoretical framework relevant to the discussion of job and career path exploration, discussion, and decision-making will offer information to consider in future public school-based recruitment and retention efforts for speech-language pathologists. There will always be facets and contributing factors that can't be controlled when considering career recruitment and retention, but it may be valuable to shift specific focus and efforts to the contributing facets that support the provision of positive influential engagement and interaction, solid opportunities for varied exposure to a multitude of speech-language pathology practice settings, and the development of continued breadth and depth of knowledge of an evolving field through discussion, practicum experiences, and interactions.

Bibliography

Bandura, A. (1977). Self-efficacy: Toward a unifying theory of behavioral change. *Psychological Review*, *84*(2), 191–215.

Bandura, A. (1986). *Social foundations of thought and action: A social cognitive theory*. Englewood Cliffs, NJ: Prentice-Hall.

Bandura, A. (2001). Social cognitive theory of mass communication. *Media Psychology*, *3*(3), 265–299.

Byrne, N. (2007). Factors influencing the selection of speech pathology as a career: A qualitative analysis utilising the systems theory framework. *Australian Journal of Career Development*, *16*, 11–18.

Hung-Bin, S., Lent, R., Brown, S., Miller, M., Hennessy, K., & Duffy, R. (2010). Testing the choice model of social cognitive career theory across Holland themes: A meta-analytic path analysis. *Journal of Vocational Behavior*, *76*, 252–264.

Kalkhoff, N. L., & Collins, D. R. (2012). Speech-language pathologist job satisfaction in school versus medical settings. *Language, Speech, and Hearing Services in Schools*, *43*, 164–175.

Lent, R. W., Brown, S. D., & Hackett, G. (1994). Toward a unifying social cognitive theory of career and academic interest, choice, and performance. *Journal of Vocational Behavior*, *45*, 79–122.

Lent, R. W., Brown, S. D., & Hackett, G. (2000). Contextual supports and barriers to career choice: A social cognitive analysis. *Journal of Counseling Psychology*, *47*(1), 36–49.

Lent, R. W., Brown, S. D., Talleyrand, R., McPartland, E., Davis, T., Chopra, S., . . . & Chai, C. (2002). Career choice barriers, supports, and coping strategies: College students' experiences. *Journal of Vocational Behavior*, *60*, 61–72.

Lunenburg, F. (2011). Expectancy theory of motivation: Motivating by altering expectations. *International Journal of Management, Business, and Administration*, *15*(1), 1–6.

Matteson, M. T., & Smith, S. V. (1977). Selection of medical specialties: Preferences versus choices. *Academic Medicine*, *52*(7), 548–554.

Merton, R. K. (1957). *Social theory and social structure*. New York, NY: Free Press.

Morgenroth, T., Ryan, M., & Peters, K. (2015). The motivational theory of role modeling: How role models influence role aspirants' goals. *Review of General Psychology*, *19*(4), 465–483.

Parijat, P., & Bagga, S. (2014). Victor Vroom's expectancy theory of motivation—an evaluation. *International Research Journal of Business and Management*, *7*(9), 1–8.

Rogers, M., & Creed, P. (2011). A longitudinal examination of adolescent career planning and exploration using a social cognitive career theory framework. *Journal of Adolescence*, *34*, 163–172.

Smith, B. K., Du, J., & Bedwinek, A. (2015). Caseload/workload study of speech-language pathologists in Missouri public schools: Implications of key factors that contribute to SLP job satisfaction. *The Online Journal of Missouri Speech-Language-Hearing Association*, *1*(1), 51–72.

Stone, L., & Pellowski, M. (2016). Factors affecting career choice among speech-language pathology and audiology students. *Communication Disorders Quarterly*, *37*(2), 100–107.

Vroom, V. H. (1964). *Work and motivation.* New York, NY: Wiley.

Whitehouse, A. J., Hird, K., & Cocks, N. (2007). The recruitment and retention of speech and language therapists: What do university students find important? *Journal of Allied Health*, *36*(3), 131–136.

4 School-Based Speech-Language Pathologist Job Satisfaction

Chapter Overview

Chapter 4, "School-Based Speech-Language Pathologist Job Satisfaction," outlines the methodology of the quantitative research study, including research questions and null hypotheses. The chapter outlines the research study's examination of the facet-based and global job satisfaction of participating Indiana, USA, speech-language pathologists employed in public-school districts or special education cooperatives. The chapter highlights the examination of the study's investigation of how predictor variables, including coworkers on the present job, work, pay, opportunities for promotion, and supervision, relate to the criterion variable of speech-language pathologists' general job satisfaction when employed full- or part-time in the public-school setting. In addition, the chapter introduces the rationale for the research design, outlining the type of study and reason for the specified research design and a description of the survey tool, including relevant reliability and validity information. Data sources, including participant eligibility and recruitment procedures, are outlined. Additionally, data collection and the method of analysis, including the statistical test and the rationale for the specified statistical test and analysis, are addressed.

***

The previous chapters have provided the literature review, theoretical constructs, and foundational knowledge to support the investigation of facet-based job satisfaction relevant to this research study. This chapter will provide the study research design, data collection procedures, and method of analysis. The quantitative study investigated the relationships among job-related facets measured by the JDI, including the JIG survey tool and job satisfaction, including

- coworkers;
- work;

- pay;
- promotion opportunities; and
- supervision.

(Bowling Green State University, 2009a)

Additionally, the research study examined the global job satisfaction measured by the JIG (Bowling Green State University, 2009b) of participating Indiana speech-language pathologists employed as practicing clinicians in public-school districts or special education cooperatives. The purpose of the study was to examine how the predictor identified variables, including coworkers on the present job, work, pay, opportunities for promotion, and supervision, relate to the criterion variable of speech-language pathologists' general job satisfaction when employed full- or part-time in the public-school setting. The study results and discussion outlined in the following chapters provide evidence and insight to help future public-school employers gain an understanding of the potential relationships between specified job facets and job satisfaction to promote employee job satisfaction impacting recruitment and retention efforts. Ultimately, this positive impact on recruitment and retention efforts has the potential to meet the speech and language needs of students in educational settings, supporting positive educational achievement specifically relevant to speech, language, and literacy acquisition, development, and use.

Understanding relationships between the predictor variables, including coworkers, work, pay, supervision, and promotion opportunities, and the criterion variable, job satisfaction, provides a foundation to assist with developing recruitment, hiring, and retention practices for school-based speech-language pathologists, based on an increased understanding of job satisfaction and significant facets. Given the high demand for speech-language pathologists and a supply that likely will not sufficiently fill the demand, information about relationships between specified job facets and overall job satisfaction has the potential to help public-school employers compete in a highly competitive speech-language pathology job market in recruitment and retention efforts.

Research Questions

The following research questions examined specific facets in relation to job satisfaction of public-school speech-language pathologists in Indiana, USA:

1. What are the current job satisfaction levels of public-school speech-language pathologists in the areas of people, work, pay, supervision, opportunities for promotion, and the job in general?

2. Do the people, work, pay, supervision, and opportunities for promotion explain a statistically significant amount of variance in the JIG score for speech-language pathologists?
3. Is there a statistically significant difference based on years of experience on the JDI composite scores for speech-language pathologists?

Null Hypotheses

The following null hypotheses examined specific facets related to job satisfaction of public-school speech-language pathologists in Indiana:

$H_0 1$: The people, work, pay, supervision, and opportunities for promotion do not explain a statistically significant amount of variance in the JIG score for speech-language pathologists.

$H_0 2$: There is no statistically significant difference based on years of experience on the JDI composite scores for speech-language pathologists.

Rationale for Research Design

This research study was quantitative, utilizing a scientifically researched survey tool, the JDI, including the JIG. Numerical data was collected to investigate the relationship between the predictor variables, including people, work, pay, supervision, and opportunities for promotion, and the criterion variable, job satisfaction. A descriptive statistical analysis was conducted to organize and summarize collected predictor and criterion variable data.

Limitations

The purpose of this quantitative study was to investigate relationships among five identified facet independent variables (people, work, pay, opportunities for promotion, and supervision) and the criterion variable of job satisfaction of public school-based speech-language pathologists employed by public-school districts and special education cooperatives in Indiana, USA. I was not able to control for introspective answers and human emotion factors. Speech-language pathologists' roles and responsibilities are complex and varied between and within school districts and special education cooperatives in Indiana. Complexity and variation may have affected the respondents' perceptions and responses, yet I did not specifically account for such complexities in this study. Speech-language pathologists employed by public-school districts and cooperatives may provide services in various settings, including public and private schools, as defined by their specific job responsibilities. Speech-language pathologists may also provide services to a diverse age group ranging from Pre-K through Grade 12. I minimized human emotional factors by using the JDI (Bowling Green State University, 2009a) and the JIG (Bowling Green State University, 2009b), researched and developed tools. Researchers have used, refined, and continually developed the survey tools over the past 50 years, making them scientifically reliable.

An additional limitation of this study was that it included only public-school districts and special education cooperatives in Indiana, whose members chose to participate. Individual participation was voluntary. I invited all speech-language pathologists employed by school districts and special education cooperatives in Indiana to participate based on access to email contact information provided by the Indiana Department of Education, using the information request process. Use of a convenience sample in Indiana may have introduced bias into the results.

Delimitations

Participation was voluntary and depended upon each individual speech-language pathologist's decision to participate in the survey. I focused this study on the specifically participating speech-language pathologists. I depended on contact information obtained from the Indiana Department of Education, using the information request process.

Survey Design

The JDI and the related JIG are based on the work and research of Smith, Kendall, and Hulin (1969). Continued research by the JDI Research Group resulted in revisions of the original JDI in 1985, 1997, and 2009. The JDI Research Group includes experts in the fields of psychology, research methods, and organizational behavior working to research workplace attitudes (Bowling Green State University, 2009a). The JDI may provide employers with information specific to necessary areas of improvement and areas of success specific to a job. Additionally, the facets are reported to provide information for predicting turnover and employee intentions to leave a job. The JDI is utilized to measure job satisfaction using specified facets, including people, work, pay, supervision, and opportunities for promotion (Bowling Green State University, 2009a). The JIG is utilized to measure an employee's overall global job satisfaction (Bowling Green State University, 2009b). The JDI and JIG are researched-based tools with ongoing study, refinement, and development based on the theoretical framework developed by Smith et al. (1969). The JDI was designed to measure job satisfaction inclusive of two subdomains, the general-long-term domain and the descriptive-specific-short-term domain (Smith et al., 1969).

Smith et al. (1969) stated job roles, organizational aspects, and leadership are considered predictors of job satisfaction. Consideration of construct validity indicated job satisfaction is a dynamic construct. Kinicki, McKee-Ryan, Schriesheim, and Carson (2002) provided supporting evidence of the revised JDI internal consistency reliability and construct validity. Reliability averages for each facet were .87 with pay, .88 with promotion, .86 with coworkers, .88 with work, and .89 with supervision for job satisfaction.

In order to investigate the relationship between the JDI job facets and general job satisfaction, the JDI and the JIG were administered to each participating public-school speech-language pathologist currently employed in the public-school environment. The JDI and the JIG were entered into Qualtrics with no modifications or adaptations to the survey instruments except for the use of an online platform for survey administration and data collection purposes.

The JDI (Bowling Green State University, 2009a) and the JIG (Bowling Green State University, 2009b) measured speech-language pathologists' satisfaction with their job related to the specified job facets. The JDI asks participants to think about and identify the words or phrases describing the specific facets of their current job and relate the identified facets to job satisfaction. The instrument consists of five facets, including satisfaction with people on present job, work on present job, pay, opportunities for promotion, and supervision. The instrument consists of 72 items, separated into nine specific items for each job facet of promotion and pay, and 18 items individualized for work, supervision, and coworkers. Each participant responded to each item within a specified facet with Y for "Yes," N for "No," or ? for "Cannot decide" according to the participant's perception of the given item.

In addition, participants completed the JIG to measure a broad global identification with job satisfaction (Bowling Green State University, 2009b). The JIG consists of 18 items to obtain information related to overall job satisfaction. Each participant responded to each item within a specified facet with Y for "Yes," N for "No," or ? for "Cannot decide" according to the participant's perception of the given item.

Participants consented to participation in the research study by means of a question built into the survey tool. Before the collection or analysis of any speech-language pathologist's data, the participant provided informed and voluntary consent. Demographic characteristics of participating speech-language pathologists were measured, including

- education level (to ensure participant eligibility);
- current professional certification (to ensure participant eligibility);
- confirmation of employment in a public-school district in Indiana, USA; and
- years of clinical experience.

No additional demographic information or IP addresses were collected. Participants answered the demographic questions before completing the JDI and JIG survey questions.

Data Sources

This research study measured job satisfaction based on participant responses on the JDI (Bowling Green State University, 2009a) specified facets and the JIG (Bowling Green State University, 2009b). All participants were employees of public-school districts in Indiana, USA. The JDI and JIG surveys were sent to 891 Indiana speech-language pathologists using email addresses provided by the Indiana Department of Education, using a public record request. Of the 891 email invitations sent, 12 emails were not valid and 11 individuals began the survey but exited because they did not meet the eligibility requirements. The study sample population consisted of a convenience sample of 91 participants, resulting in a 10% overall return rate.

The surveyed speech-language pathologists were full- or part-time employees in a public-school district or special education cooperative in Indiana. Speech-language pathology students, speech-language pathology assistants and aides, and unemployed speech-language pathologists did not participate in the study. Clinical Fellowship Year (CFY) speech-language pathologists were invited to participate in the research study. Participating speech-language pathologists were required to hold an Indiana speech-language pathology license with the Indiana Professional Licensing Agency (IPLA) but did not need to hold an ASHA Certificate of Clinical Competence. Participants who did not complete both the JDI (Bowling Green State University, 2009a) and the JIG (Bowling Green State University, 2009b) were excluded from the study. The participating licensed and employed school-based speech-language pathologists were all 18 years of age or older and had the ability to read and write in English.

Data Collection Methods and Data Procedures

Eligible participants had two weeks to complete the survey. The acquired data was exported from Qualtrics to SPSS version 24. Coding was checked to ensure accuracy of demographics and survey responses. Composite scores were created for each predictor variable found with inferential testing, including people, work, pay, supervision, opportunities for promotion, and job in general. After the composite scores were created, descriptive and inferential testing was run. The final analysis of the data reported aggregate data and overall trends.

Method of Analysis

The study's data were analyzed using descriptive statistics and simultaneous multiple regression for determining relationships between predictor variables people, work, pay, supervision, and opportunities for promotion and a criterion variable, job satisfaction. Descriptive statistics organized and summarized collected interval scale data to address the current job satisfaction levels of public-school speech-language pathologists, including the areas of people, work, pay, supervision, opportunities for promotion, and the job in general. Data were summarized using measures of central tendency, including the mean, median, and mode. Range, variance, and standard deviation were utilized for the purpose of description of the distribution of numerical data in relation to variation. Variance and standard deviation were used to show the difference between the raw score and the distribution mean.

Simultaneous multiple regression was used to determine if the people, work, pay, supervision, and opportunities for promotion facets explained a statistically significant variance in the JIG score. Additionally, the statistical analysis addressed the statistical significance of the facets when years of experience were considered. Multiple regression, a correlation statistic, analyzed relationships among multiple variables. A regression statistical analysis was used to determine the relationship between the combination of predictor variables and the criterion variable, the multiple correlation coefficient. Regression assumes variables are normally distributed; a linear relationship between the predictor and criterion variables; no multicollinearity, meaning the predictor variables are not highly correlated with each other; and homoscedasticity, assuming the error variance is similar across levels of the predictor variables (Osborne & Waters, 2002). Linearity, homogeneity, normality, independence, and multicollinearity were checked to avoid Type I errors, overestimation resulting in rejection of a null hypothesis that is true, and Type II errors, resulting in not rejecting a null hypothesis that is false (Field, 2013).

Model summary statistics were interpreted to determine the relationship strength. Linear combination of the predictor variables was analyzed to determine if the combined predictor variables explain significance of variance in the criterion variable. A *t*-test was used to determine which predictor variables were significant. An unstandardized partial regression coefficient was used to determine change predicted in the criterion variable with a one-unit increase in the specific predictor variable while holding all other variables constant. Additionally, a standardized partial regression coefficient determined the rank order of the predictor variables if two or more of the predictor variables were significant.

An analysis of variance (ANOVA) statistical test was completed to determine if there was a significant difference on any of the specified facets or JIG scores based on the respondent's years of experience. An individual ANOVA statistical test was run for each of the specified facets with consideration of each years of experience subgroup. The assumptions of the ANOVA statistical test, including normality, ensuring scores with subgroups are normally distributed, and homogeneity of variance, were explained by all variances in each subgroup being equal. Post hoc comparisons using Tukey's honest significant difference test were conducted to examine differences among JDI facets for years of experience subgroups because significance was found based on ANOVA statistical analysis.

The following chapters will provide study results in relation to the specified research questions associated with this study. Results will offer insight to support continued discussion of facet-based job satisfaction and the impact on recruitment and retention. Additionally, exploration of job satisfaction associated with years of experience provides a platform for development and implementation of strategies for supporting speech-language pathologists in establishing and maintaining individual and collective job satisfaction at all stages of their career. Additionally, the research-to-practice connection supporting ongoing discussions and systemic considerations to support speech-language pathologists practicing within school settings is discussed.

Bibliography

Bowling Green State University. (2009a). *The Job Descriptive Index 2009 revision*. Retrieved from www.bgsu.edu/arts-and-sciences/psychology/services/job-descriptive-index.html

Bowling Green State University. (2009b). *The Job in General scale*. Retrieved from www.bgsu.edu/arts-and-sciences/psychology/services/job-descriptive-index.html

Field, A. (2013). *Discovering statistics using IBM SPSS statistics* (4th ed.). London, England: SAGE.

Kinicki, A. J., McKee-Ryan, F. M., Schriesheim, C. A., & Carson, K. (2002). Assessing the construct validity of the job descriptive index: A review and meta-analysis. *Journal of Applied Psychology, 87*(1), 14–32.

Osborne, J., & Waters, E. (2002). Four assumptions of multiple regression that researchers should always test. *Practical Assessment, Research, and Evaluation, 8*(2), 1–5.

Smith, P. C., Kendall, L. M., & Hulin, C. L. (1969). *The measurement of satisfaction in work and retirement*. Chicago, IL: Rand McNally.

5 Facet-Based Job Satisfaction

Chapter Overview

Chapter 5, "Facet-Based Job Satisfaction," focuses on the relationship between specified facets, including people, work, pay, opportunities for promotion, and supervision, and speech-language pathologists' general job satisfaction through whole sample and subgroup data analysis. In order to analyze the results of the completed study, the chapter discusses various definitions and associated information related to job satisfaction. Additional information identifies the components of organizational culture impacting job satisfaction. After providing summarized results specific to each facet for the whole sample, results are provided for each subgroup followed by a comparison to whole sample data. Considerations and implications of data analysis and discussion provide insights for administrators, specifically focused on work, supervision, and pay, the facets identified as significant based on study results.

***

Chapter 4 provided a comprehensive outline of this research study's design, administration, and statistical analysis. In order to analyze the results of the completed study, it is beneficial to ensure a strong understanding of job satisfaction, including career and job satisfaction. Kinicki, McKee, and Wade (1996) cited job satisfaction as the most frequently researched dependent variable in occupational health. Studying multiple definitions of job satisfaction reveals various factors that may affect a person's perceptions about and feelings toward a specific job (Boynton & McDaniel, 2020). The majority of job satisfaction definitions are linked by similarities based on positive feelings toward meeting a person's need for work-related fulfillment. Vroom (1964) stated job satisfaction is a positive attitude related to the role a person currently occupies. Researchers have identified job satisfaction as a related aspect of improved performance; improved work ethic and motivation; and reduction of employee absences, turnover, and burnout (Begley & Czajka, 1993). The measurement of job satisfaction has gained increased scientific and practice-based relevance, resulting from evidence that there is indeed a relationship between job satisfaction and an organization's employee attendance, work performance, and work-related stress (Berry, 1998).

ASHA utilized the Omnibus Surveys for more than 20 years to determine speech-language pathologist career and job satisfaction. ASHA (2004) offers a distinction between career and job satisfaction, defining *career satisfaction* as the level of satisfaction based on an individual's career choice. Alternatively, *job satisfaction* is dependent upon an individual's current work situation and aspects of a specific employment situation. Career satisfaction and job satisfaction may contribute in combined or separate ways to overall work-life balance and enjoyment. The possibility that a person may experience career satisfaction in the absence of job satisfaction is a potential reality for some individuals. This concept provides an opportunity to pause and thoughtfully consider the reason why speech-language pathologists make the choice to leave school settings for other settings, resign from a position at one local school district to work for another local school district in a neighboring community, or request a transfer from one school to another within a school district. In these cases, perhaps the speech-language pathologist has career satisfaction, but is lacking job satisfaction; that is, enjoys the practice of speech-language pathology, but is unable to find positive satisfaction within the current job situation. Of course, we can't minimize the role of pay as a potential factor for changing employment settings or leaving one district for another, but perhaps it would be helpful to ponder if there are other factors that may be contributing to these job transfers and changes. As educational leaders, determining the root cause of these changes and requests would offer insight into potential systemic changes to promote retention efforts and ensure individuals are matched with the best job placement possible within an individual's scope of practice.

Job satisfaction researchers identify two job satisfaction aspects for study: facet-based job satisfaction and overall general job satisfaction (Cherrington, 1994). Facet-based job satisfaction is an employee's tendency to feel varying degrees of satisfaction depending on distinct facets or aspects of a job (Johns, 1988). Overall job satisfaction is a general satisfaction or dissatisfaction from within a person related to the job (Suma & Lesha, 2013). Pezzei and Oratio (1991) suggested job satisfaction is defined by intrinsic and extrinsic aspects, including professional growth, personal job interest, and job responsibilities. This information allows us the opportunity to identify ways to support current and future speech-language pathologists in achieving individual and collective professional growth through mentorship, meaningful goal development and evaluation, and collaborative, collegial learning opportunities. Wisniewski and Gargiulo (1997) found that one extrinsic factor, high caseloads, increased stress and burnout and decreased school-based speech-language pathologist job satisfaction. The negative impact has the potential to affect both the well-being of the speech-language pathologist and the progress of students served. There is potential value in investigating service delivery models and tiered intervention approaches for support students and providing collaborative practice, including Response to Intervention (RTI) and Multi-tiered Systems of Support (MTSS). It is imperative to consider the impact of stress and burnout on both the professionals providing the services and the students receiving support in order to achieve the most rewarding outcomes for students, while sustaining a speech-language pathologist's commitment to the field, including the motivation to seek ongoing professional growth. Indeed, it is important to support the speech-language pathologist in maintaining work-related happiness and fulfillment, while taking into significant consideration a work and life balance.

Hutchins, Howard, Prelock, and Belin (2010) established as fact the growing national school-based speech-language pathologist shortage. Harris, Prater, Dyches, and Heath (2009) found that stress and burnout affect speech-language pathologist retention and job satisfaction in public schools. Blood, Thomas, Ridenour, Qualls, and Hammer (2002) asserted that job stress is a major problem confronting school professionals. Public schools experience a continuous struggle to recruit and retain certified speech-language pathologists. Despite the consensus that stress and burnout are a problem, few researchers have studied factors contributing to public-school professionals' stress and burnout (Harris et al., 2009).

According to Edgar and Rosa-Lugo (2007), school-based speech-language pathologists in Florida reported the most positive aspect of school-based work is the opportunity to work with children within an educational setting during school hours. Less favorable factors included workload, caseload, unclear responsibilities definition, and pay. The study identified positive and negative factors that may increase attrition and compound the potential for school-based recruitment challenges.

In addition to high caseloads, school-based speech-language pathologists have increasing and evolving responsibilities. The responsibilities include administrative responsibilities, increased paperwork mandates, and increased expectation of collaboration with other professionals (ASHA, 2004). Awareness and knowledge of these increased job roles and responsibilities may deter speech-language pathologists from entering into employment opportunities in the school setting. I find it beneficial to continue asking the question of how we can find ways to offer insight, perspective, and a glimpse into ways to effectively manage these potentially deterring factors before speech-language pathologists reach a point of burnout or before they rule out the possibility of working in a school-based setting.

Potter and Lagace (1995) surveyed school-based speech-language pathologists and found that 76% experienced mild to moderate burnout, defined by physical and mental exhaustion that caused negative job attitudes. Potter and Lagace identified a significant relationship among professional burnout and job satisfaction. Similarly, Kaegi, Svitich, Chambers, Bakker, and Schneider (2002) surveyed speech-language pathologists in three regions in Canada, including urban and rural areas, and the majority of survey participants reported that burnout resulted from increased caseload size and negative workplace change. The Coordinating Committee of the Vice President for Speech-Language Pathology Practice (2009) indicated a common trend of increased caseloads and paperwork that negatively impact speech-language pathologists' job satisfaction. Additional evidence of the factors linked to job satisfaction and dissatisfaction can be found within the research follow-up questions to the 2004 Omnibus Survey. Researchers identified the major causes of job dissatisfaction, including paperwork, salary or benefit reduction, increased caseload, and increased service sites (Zingeser, 2004). In the 2003 Omnibus Survey, participants identified the top three factors contributing to job satisfaction: setting, pay, and collaborative working relationships. I want to highlight the potential role of collaborative working relationships in conjunction with the previously mentioned service delivery and tiered intervention support systems. If speech-language pathologists' job satisfaction is positively impacted by collaborative working relationships, it seems beneficial to consider ways to support opportunities for promoting a collaborative work environment with a focus on supporting students, professional growth, and shared professional roles and responsibilities.

It is important to note that job satisfaction results have lacked a similar level of consistency over several years of surveying. The levels of job satisfaction and the contributing factors related to global job satisfaction have varied over survey years (Zingeser, 2004). Although the surveys indicated a consistent level of career satisfaction, fluctuating levels of job satisfaction are evident. It is notable that all speech-language pathologists surveyed worked within healthcare settings, including medical, rehabilitation, and pediatric hospitals; skilled nursing facilities; home healthcare; and outpatient or speech and hearing clinics (ASHA, 2004). The roles, responsibilities, organizational environment, and collaborative opportunities often differ in structure and function when comparing medical and educational settings. It is important to note that the included facet-based research study is specific to speech-language pathology practice within the school-based setting. The focus of the study offers a window into perceptions linked to school-based practice with a goal of inspiring school leaders and speech-language pathologists to engage in meaningful discussion to build and enhance job satisfaction.

It is also important to recognize and mention that speech-language pathology roles and responsibilities have grown to include diverse populations within a multitude of settings (Leonard, Plexico, Plumb, & Sandage, 2016). Given the evolving scope of practice, expansion of literacy involvement, and practice spanning a wide landscape, we need to continue to study and gain a deeper understanding of the opportunities, barriers, rewards, and frustrations embedded and interwoven in school-based practice. Although it is valuable to research and understand global job satisfaction across multiple settings, limited studies have focused on facet-based job satisfaction, potentially leading to a gap in understanding ways to support school-based speech-language pathologists in effective and meaningful ways. The growing diversity of the speech-language pathology field makes it more important than ever to study the unique needs of local speech-language pathologists in Indiana, specifically focused on job facets.

Finn (2001) suggested there are specific intrinsic and extrinsic facets linked to job satisfaction in the field of nursing. The research specific to practicing nurses may offer insight into the study of speech-language pathologists. Finn found that positive relationships along with autonomous work environments, involvement in decision-making, pay, and job status had positive effects on job satisfaction. Al-Swidi, Nawawi, and Al-Hosam (2012) noted individuals in academia, as well as clinical practitioners, agreed on four factors that determine job satisfaction levels: the team makeup, autonomous work environment, type of leadership, and type of work. Additionally, Randolph (2005) studied the intrinsic and extrinsic aspects related to job satisfaction of speech-language pathologists, occupational therapists, and physical therapists practicing within a rehabilitation setting. The research results showed that intrinsic factors had a greater impact than extrinsic factors when predicting job satisfaction and willingness to remain in a role at a current job. Speech-language pathologists participating in the study identified career accomplishments, manageable workload, support staff, work and home balance, schedule flexibility, and helping individuals with disabilities as predictive of career satisfaction. In addition, predictors of a speech-language pathologist's desire to remain at a current job included schedule flexibility, appropriate training, manageable workload, and lack of role conflict. Although the study obtained data from speech-language pathologists in the rehabilitation setting, similar intrinsic and extrinsic job and career satisfaction factors may be a consideration for publicschool speech-language pathologists.

In considering the impact of job satisfaction, we may also benefit from understanding the role and impact of job satisfaction on early experiences of speech-language pathology students and early career clinicians. Public school-based speech-language pathologists with higher job satisfaction rates may provide more positive mentoring experiences for new clinicians and encourage speech-language pathology students to consider working in school-based settings after graduation. Ensuring more positive interactions may allow for stronger recruitment and retention strategies, which has the potential to positively impact the success of both the professional providing service and the students receiving speech and language services. In addition, an understanding of known barriers, challenges, and stressors in the Pre-K through Grade 12 setting may enable school districts to design additional strategies for supporting both new and experienced speech-language pathologists in their current positions with ongoing professional growth potential and opportunities for systemic educational contributions. Support within a healthy work environment may promote and maintain job satisfaction and reduce unnecessary job stress, making public school-based speech-language pathology opportunities a more attractive career path. The following data provides insight into the impact of specified facets on overall job satisfaction based on the developed and implemented research study.

Whole Sample Descriptive Data

The outlined information summarizes the results of two research questions investigated in this study related to the specified facets, including people, work, pay, supervision, opportunities for promotion, and job in general. These two research questions investigated the current job satisfaction within the specified facets and explored the statistical significance of the amount of variance in the JIG score. Of the 91 speech-language pathologist respondents, 21 (23.1%) had less than five years of experience, 16 (17.6%) had six to ten years, 24 (26.4%) had 10 to 20 years, and 30 (33.0%) had more than 21 years. Whole sample data analysis indicated particular attributes were specific to individual facets. The data is presented first as a whole sample and subgroup data will follow.

People

Based on whole sample analysis of the people facet, data indicated an overall higher percentage linked to positive attributes (*stimulating, helpful, responsible, likable, intelligent, smart, supportive,* and *active*) compared to negative attributes (*boring, slow, stupid, easy to make enemies, rude, lazy, unpleasant, narrow interests, frustrating,* and *stubborn*). When asked about specific

50 *Facet-Based Job Satisfaction*

positive attributes describing people with whom participants worked, 93.4% of participants reported people they work with are *smart*, 93.4% *likable*, 92.3% *intelligent*, 91.2% *responsible*, 89.0% *helpful*, 83.5% *stimulating*, 82.4% *supportive*, and 79.1% *active*. Based on responses, participants identified the highest percentage linked to the positive attributes *smart, likable, intelligent*, and *responsible* when describing current colleagues.

Work

Whole sample data analysis of the work facet indicated an overall higher percentage of association linked to positive attributes (*fascinating, satisfying, good, sense of accomplishment, respected, exciting, rewarding, useful, creative, can see results*, and *uses my abilities*) in comparison to negative attributes (*routine, boring, challenging, repetitive, dull*, and *uninteresting*). Respondents indicated association with positive attributes, with 94.5% reporting their current work as *useful*, 92.3% *rewarding*, 91.2% *good*, 87.9% *uses my abilities*, 86.8% *provides a sense of accomplishment*, 85.7% *can see results*, 83.5% *satisfying*, 74.7% *creative*, 57.1% *fascinating*, 53.8% *respected*, and 50.5% *exciting*. Based on responses, participants identified the highest percentage linked to the positive attributes *useful, rewarding, good*, and *uses my abilities*. Participants chose *challenging* equally to *provides a sense of accomplishment* at 86.8%, and *challenging* exceeded additional positive attribute percentages.

Pay

Whole sample data analysis of the pay facet indicated an overall variation of percentages of positive attributes (*adequate to cover normal expenses, fair, comfortable, well paid*, and *enough to live on*) compared to negative attributes (*barely live on income, bad, less than I deserve*, and *underpaid*). Highest attribute percentage identification with regard to pay included 84.6% of respondents reporting *less than I deserve* and 82.4% reporting *underpaid*. Only 59.3% indicated current pay was *enough to live on*, and 47.3% reported *adequate for normal expenses*.

Opportunities for Promotion

Whole sample data analysis of the opportunities for promotion facet indicated higher percentages of negative attributes (*somewhat limited, dead-end job, very limited*, and *infrequent promotions*) compared to positive attributes (*good opportunity, promotion on ability, good chance, regular promotions*, and *fairly good chance*). When asked about opportunities for job promotion, 94.5% of participants reported they did not feel there were good opportunities. An equal percentage of respondents, 94.5%, reported opportunities for promotion as *somewhat limited*. Additionally, 91.2% of respondents indicated *infrequent promotions*, 86.8% indicated *very limited* opportunities for promotion, and 52.7% viewed their current job as a *dead end*. Conversely, 94.5% reported a lack of perceived *good opportunities* for promotion, 92.3% indicated a lack of *regular promotions*, and 89.0% reported they did not believe there were fairly good chances for *promotional opportunities*.

Supervision

Whole sample data analysis of the supervision facets indicated varied perceptions related to current supervision based on positive attributes (*supportive, praises good work, tactful, influential, up to date, tells me where I stand, knows the job well, intelligent,* and *around when needed*) compared to negative attributes (*hard to please, impolite, unkind, has favorites, annoying, stubborn, bad, poor planner,* and *lazy*). When asked about current supervision, 83.5% of participants described current supervisors as *intelligent*, 78.0% *tactful*, 73.6% *supportive*, and 67.0% reported *praises good work*. Conversely, only 45.1% reported that current supervisors *know the job well*, and 41.8% indicated a perception that current supervisors *have favorites*.

Job in General

Whole sample data analysis indicated an overall positive perception of the job in general, based on the participants' selection of positive attributes (*pleasant, great, good, worthwhile, acceptable, superior, better than most, makes me content,* and *excellent*) compared to negative attributes (*bad, waste of time, undesirable, worse than most, disagreeable, inadequate,* and *poor*). When asked about the job in general, 93.4% of respondents indicated the job is *pleasant* and *acceptable*, 90.1% reported their job in general is *good*, and 85.7% reported it *worthwhile*. Additionally, 64.8% of respondents reported the job *makes them content*, and 62.6% reported the job is *better than most*. Conversely, only 34.1% reported the job in general is *excellent*, and 25.3% indicated the job is *superior*.

Descriptive Data for Less Than Five Years

The following section contains descriptive data for speech-language pathologist participants with less than five years' experience for each of the five JDI facets and the JIG instrument. For each facet, the researcher compared data from the whole sample to the data specific to this subgroup. Of the 91 speech-language pathologists who participated in the study, 21 (23.1%) had less than five years' experience.

People

Compared to the whole sample data analysis related to the specific JDI people facet, speech-language pathologists with less than five years of experience indicated overall consistent perceptions with positive and negative attributes. Comparison of the specific positive attributes indicated a 6.6% increase in speech-language pathologists with less than five years of experience who perceive the people they work with to be *smart*. Additionally, compared to whole sample data, 6.2% more speech-language pathologists in this subgroup reported a perception that people with whom they work are *stubborn*. Overall perception was associated with positive attributes more than negative attributes, which is consistent with whole data sample findings.

Work

Compared to the whole sample data analysis related to the specific JDI work facet, speech-language pathologists with less than five years of experience indicated an increase in positive attributes. Comparison of the specific attributes indicated a 19.1% increase in speech-language pathologists with less than five years of experience perceiving that the work they do is *fascinating* compared to the sample as a whole. Additionally, 20.9% more speech-language pathologists in this category, with regards to work, reported a perception that the work they do is *exciting* compared to the whole sample data.

Pay

Compared to the whole sample data analysis related to the specific JDI pay facet, speech-language pathologists with less than five years of experience indicated an increase specific to the negative attributes *bad* and *less than I deserve* regarding pay received. Comparison of the specific attributes indicated that perception that the pay received is bad is 8.0% higher among speech-language pathologists with less than five years of experience than among the whole sample. Additionally, 10.6% more speech-language pathologists with less than five years of experience reported a perception that the pay is *less than deserved* compared to the whole sample data.

Opportunities for Promotion

Compared to the whole sample data analysis related to the specific JDI opportunities for promotion facet, speech-language pathologists with less than five years of experience indicated an increase in opportunities for promotion *based on ability* and a decrease in perception of *dead-end* opportunities for promotion. Comparison of the specific attributes indicated a 6.6% increase in speech-language pathologists with less than five years of experience perceiving that opportunities for promotion are *based on ability*. Additionally, there was a 14.6% decrease among participants in this subgroup in perception that *dead end* described opportunities for promotion compared to the sample as a whole.

Supervision

Compared to the whole sample data analysis related to the specific JDI the supervision facet, speech-language pathologists with less than five years of experience indicated an increase in perception of positive attributes in supervisors. Specific differences included a 16.9% increase in perception that supervisors are *supportive* compared to the whole sample data, a 14.0% increase in perception that supervisors *praise hard work*, a 17.2% increase in perception that supervisors are *influential*, a 17.9% increase in perception that supervisors are *up to date*, a 21.6% increase in perception that supervisors *know the job well*, and a 19.1% increase in perception that supervisors are *around when needed*. Additionally, related to negative attributes, there was a 6.2% decrease in participants in this category reporting that the supervisor is *hard to please*, a 12.1% decrease in reporting that the supervisor is *annoying*, and a 7.3% decrease in reporting that the supervisor is *stubborn*.

Job in General

Compared to the whole sample data analysis related to the specific JDI job in general facet, speech-language pathologists with less than five years of experience identified increased positive perceptions of the job in general. Comparison of the specific attributes indicated a 9.5% increase in perception that the job in general is *worthwhile*. Additionally, when asked if the job was *superior*, there was an increase of 17.6% in affirmative responses compared to the whole sample data.

Descriptive Data for Six to Ten Years

The following section contains descriptive data for speech-language pathologist participants with experience equal to six to ten years for each of the

JDI facets and the JIG instrument. Of the 91 speech-language pathologists who participated in the study, 16 (17.6 %) had six to ten years' experience. Data in this subgroup is also compared to the whole sample findings.

People

Compared to the whole sample data analysis related to the specific JDI people facet, speech-language pathologists with six to ten years of experience indicated an increase in negative attributes perceived. Comparison of the specific negative attributes indicated a 13.3% increase among participants in this subgroup in the perception that people with whom they work are *lazy*. Additionally, there was an 8.1% increase in *unpleasant*, a 15.9% increase in *frustrating*, and a 7.4% increase in *stubborn*. Additionally, this subgroup showed a 16.6% decrease in perception that people with whom respondents work are *active*.

Work

Compared to the whole sample data analysis related to the specific JDI work facet, speech-language pathologists with six to ten years of experience identified a decrease in the attributes of *satisfaction* and *excitement*. Comparison of the specific attributes indicated a 13.0% decrease in respondents choosing *exciting* related to current work and a 13.8% decrease in identifying the work as *fascinating*. Additionally, respondents reported a 14.7% decrease in perception that current work is *satisfying*.

Pay

Compared to the whole sample data analysis related to the specific JDI pay facet, speech-language pathologists with six to ten years of experience indicated similar perceptions related to the pay facet. Comparisons between the whole sample and the filtered sample indicated a perception that pay is *less than deserved*. Additionally, speech-language pathologist respondents reported perceptions of being *underpaid*. When asked if pay was *fair*, 15.7% fewer respondents in this subgroup responded affirmatively in comparison to the whole sample. This subgroup indicated a 9.5% increase in the perception that pay is *enough to live* on than did the sample as a whole.

Opportunities for Promotion

Compared to the whole sample data analysis related to the specific JDI opportunities for promotion facet, speech-language pathologists with six to ten years of experience indicated perceptual variation. Comparison of the specific attributes indicated change of perception related to opportunities for promotion among participants with six to ten years of experience. Among participants with six to ten years of experience, there was a 9.2% increase in respondents who perceived there are *good opportunities* for promotion compared to the sample as a whole. Despite this increase, 100% of respondents in this subgroup identified the opportunities as *somewhat limited*. This subgroup also indicated an 11.1% increase over the whole sample in the perception that promotions are *based on ability*. Additionally, respondents identified a 15.2% increase in the perception that speech-language pathology promotion opportunities are a *dead end* and a 9.9% increase in the perception that promotions are *infrequent*.

Supervision

Compared to the whole sample data analysis related to the specific JDI supervision facet, speech-language pathologists with six to ten years of experience reported both an increase and a decrease in various attributes linked to supervision. Based on comparison to whole sample data, speech-language pathologists with six to ten years of experience indicated a 4.7% decrease with *hard to please* and a 9.5% decrease with *tactful*, and 13.5% fewer speech-language pathologists perceived supervisors as *poor planners*. In addition, there was a 13.0% increase in the perception that supervision was *influential*. The most significant variation was a 23.6% decrease related to supervisors telling the speech-language pathologist where the latter stands. Fewer respondents reported supervisors to *have favorites* (10.5%).

Job in General

Compared to the whole sample data analysis related to the specific JDI job in general facet, speech-language pathologists with six to ten years of experience reported a decreased perception of positive attributes and increased perception of negative attributes linked to the job in general. Respondents reported an 8.1% increase in identification of the job in general as *undesirable* and a 16.9% decrease in perception of the job as *worthwhile*. In addition, respondents identified the job in general with a 12.6% decrease in relation to the positive attribute *better than most*.

Descriptive Data for 10 to 20 Years

The following section contains descriptive data for speech-language pathologist participants with experience equal to 10 to 20 years, showing the data relating to the five facets of the JDI and job satisfaction measured by the JIG instrument. Of the 91 speech-language pathologists who participated in the study, 24 (26.3%) had 10 to 20 years of experience. For each facet, comparisons of the data to the whole sample findings are summarized.

People

Compared to the whole sample data analysis related to the specific JDI people facet, speech-language pathologists with 10 to 20 years of experience indicated a decrease in the negative perception of the people with whom they work. Respondents identified a 5.5% decrease in the perception that people with whom they worked are *lazy*, a 7.9% decrease in the perception of *narrow interests*, and a 7.1% decrease in identifying coworkers as *frustrating*. In addition, compared to whole sample data, there was a 5.1% decrease in the perception that people with whom respondents work are *stubborn*.

Work

Compared to the whole sample data analysis related to the specific JDI work facet, speech-language pathologists with 10 to 20 years of experience indicated a decrease in several positive perception attributes. Comparison of the specific attributes indicated a 19.6% decrease in identification of work as fascinating and a 13.0% decrease in *exciting*. In addition, there was a 17.3% decrease in the identification of work as rewarding and a 20.1% decrease in *challenging*. Respondents also reported a decrease of 10.7% in seeing results based on work and a 21.2% decrease in the perception that current work used the individual's abilities.

Pay

Compared to the whole sample data analysis related to the specific JDI pay facet, speech-language pathologists with 10 to 20 years of experience indicated a decrease of 9.5% in responses that pay is *fair*. Based on responses, 0% of survey respondents reported they are *well-paid*, which was a 4.4% decrease compared to the whole sample data. Respondents in this subgroup exhibited a 7.1% increase compared to the sample as a whole in responding that pay is *less than deserved*.

Opportunities for Promotion

Compared to the whole sample data analysis related to the specific JDI opportunities for promotion facet, speech-language pathologists with 10 to 20 years of experience indicated minimal variation and increased consistency regarding positive and negative attributes related to opportunities for promotion. Respondents identified consistent perceptions, including a slight increase in considering opportunities *somewhat limited*, in comparison to the whole sample data (94.5%). Respondents also consistently perceived opportunities for promotion to be *infrequent* and *very limited*.

Supervision

Compared to the whole sample data analysis related to the specific JDI supervision facet, speech-language pathologists with 10 to 20 years of experience reported an increase in the perceptions that supervision is linked to positive attributes, including a 15.4% increase in *around when needed*. Based on data comparison, more significant variation was indicated by an increase in negative attributes, including a 17.1% increase in the perception that supervisors are *stubborn* and *annoying*. In addition, there was a 6.9% decrease in supervisors perceived as *supportive* and a 12.0% decrease in *influential*.

Job in General

Compared to the whole sample data analysis related to the specific JDI job in general facet, speech-language pathologists with 10 to 20 years of experience indicated a decrease in positive perceptions of the job in general. Respondents in this subgroup reported a 19.0% decrease in perception that the job in general is *great*, a 10.7% decrease in *worthwhile*, a 17.0% decrease in *superior*, and a 16.8% decrease in identification of the job as *better than most*. Additionally, there was a 14.8% decrease in the identification of the job in general as making the speech-language pathologist *content*.

Descriptive Data for More Than 21 Years

The following section contains descriptive data for speech-language pathologist survey participants with experience equal to 21 or more years related to the JDI five job facets and job satisfaction measured by the JIG instrument. Of the 91 speech-language pathologists who participated in the study, 30 (33.0%) had more than 21 years' experience. Data in this subgroup is also compared to the whole sample findings.

People

Compared to the whole sample data analysis related to the specific JDI people facet, speech-language pathologists with 21 or more years of experience indicated a decrease in perception of negative attributes. Positive attribute percentages were consistent with minimal variation compared to whole sample data. Respondents indicated a 5.4% decrease in the perception that people with whom they work are *frustrating* and a 4.3% decrease in relationship to *stubborn* compared to the sample as a whole.

Work

Compared to the whole sample data analysis related to the specific JDI work facet, speech-language pathologists with 21 or more years of experience indicated an increase in positive attributes. Comparison of the specific attributes indicated a 9.6% increase in perception of work as *fascinating* and an 11.0% increase in *seeing results*. In addition, 100% of respondents identified current work as *rewarding* and *useful*.

Pay

Compared to the whole sample data analysis related to the specific JDI pay facet, speech-language pathologists with 21 or more years of experience indicated a decrease in the perception of pay being *less than deserved* and of being *underpaid*. Based on responses, there was an 11.3% decrease in the perception of pay being *less than deserved*. Additionally, responses indicated a 9.1% decrease in the perception of being *underpaid*.

Opportunities for Promotion

Compared to the whole sample data analysis related to the specific JDI opportunities for promotion facet, speech-language pathologists with 21 or more years of experience indicated consistent perceptions. Perceptions included opportunities *somewhat* and *very limited*. Additionally, opportunities for promotion were perceived as *infrequent*.

Supervision

Compared to the whole sample data analysis related to the specific JDI supervision facet, speech-language pathologists with 21 or more years of experience reported a 9.0% increase in perception that supervisors are *hard to please.* Related to this perception, there was a reported 10.3% decrease in the perception that supervisors *praise good work.* Respondents in this subgroup reported a 10.7% decrease in the perception that supervisors are *up –to date* and an 8.4% decrease in *knows the job well.*

Job in General

Compared to the whole sample data analysis related to the specific JDI job in general facet, speech-language pathologists with 21 or more years of experience identified with increased positive perception of the job in general. Respondents reported increased perception of the job in general as *good*, with a 6.6% reported increase over the sample as a whole; *worthwhile*, with an 11.0% increase; and *better than most*, with a 17.4% increase. Respondents reported a 5.9% increase in the perception that the job in general is *excellent* compared to whole sample data.

Analysis of Statistical Significance

In addition to descriptive statistical analysis, examination of whether the specified facets, including people, work, pay, supervision, and opportunities for promotion, explained a statistically significant variance in the JIG score was completed. The null hypothesis, $H_0 1$: The people, work, pay, supervision, and opportunities for promotion do not explain a statistically significant amount of variance in the JIG score for speech-language pathologists, was tested using a simultaneous multiple regression statistical test and used the regression statistical analysis to determine the relationships among the combined predictor variables and the criterion variable. The assumptions were examined within a multiple regression statistical test, including linearity, homogeneity, normality, independence, and multicollinearity, to ensure all assumptions were met or correction was made if violations occurred.

All assumptions were met, ensuring normal distribution of variables, a linear relationship between predictor and criterion variables, predictor variables not highly correlated, and similar error variance across predictor variables. The assumption of linearity was examined to ensure a linear relationship between the X and Y variables. All residuals fell within the 95% confidence bands around zero, meeting the linearity assumption. The assumption of multicollinearity was met with tolerance levels for all predictor variables, including people, work, pay, promotion, and supervision, above the .2 minimum needed for the assumption. The tolerance levels ranged from a low of .717 to a high of .884. Examination of the assumption of independence was met because no systematic pattern was present on the plot of residuals. The distribution of residual data points on the probability plot met the assumption of normality. The residual data points were the same across all values of X, meeting the assumption of homogeneity of variance.

The multiple correlation coefficient showed the linear combined relationship of the predictor variables, people, work, pay, opportunities for promotion, and supervision, to the JIG. A multiple correlation coefficient of .593 indicated a strong relationship between the linear combination of the predictor variables and the criterion variable. The coefficient of multiple determination is the amount of variance within the JIG that can be explained by the linear composite of the five predictor facets. The coefficient of multiple determination value of .352 indicated the linear composite of the five predictor variables explained 35.2% of the variance within the JIG. The adjusted coefficient of multiple determination, adjusted $R^2 = .314$, provided an estimate for the coefficient of determination for the population with a correction based on the number of predictor variables in relation to the sample size. The linear composite of the five predictor variables explained 31.4% of the variance with a correction based on number of predictors and sample size. The 3.8% difference was the shrinkage within the model. The standard error of the estimate measured the average distance each data point fell from the regression line within the distribution. The model had a standard deviation of 7.36 units of the distance of residuals from the regression line.

The one-way ANOVA indicated JDI facets can be used to determine a significant difference on the JIG score based on participant years of experience. The one-way ANOVA was significant, $F(5, 85) = 9.23$, $p < .001$, demonstrating at least one level of the independent variable, years of experience, was significantly different than another level of the JIG score. The model indicated three predictors (JDI facets) significantly predicted job satisfaction: work, pay, and supervision. Work was a significant predictor of job satisfaction, $t(5, 85) = 2.647$, $p = .010$. Pay was a significant predictor of job satisfaction, $t(5, 85) = 2.004$, $p = .048$. Supervision was a significant predictor of job satisfaction, $t(5, 85) = 2.317$, $p = .023$.

The multiple regression indicated the predictor facets (people, work, pay, opportunities for promotion, and supervision) have the ability to predict general job satisfaction measured by the JIG. Significant predictor facets included work, supervision, and pay. In the following paragraph, I outline strength of significance based on a one-unit increase, while holding all other predictor variables constant.

Work had an unstandardized partial regression coefficient of .221, indicating that for a one-unit increase on the work facet score, the JIG is predicted to increase by .22 points, while holding all other predictor variables constant. With a .26 standardized partial regression coefficient, the work facet score was the strongest of the significant predictors within the model. Supervision had an unstandardized partial regression coefficient of .171, indicating that for a one-unit increase on the supervision facet score, the JIG is predicted to increase by .17 points, while holding all other predictor variables constant. With a .22 standardized partial regression coefficient, the supervision facet score was the second strongest significant predictor within the model. Pay had an unstandardized partial regression coefficient of .210, indicating that for a one-unit increase on the pay facet score, the JIG is predicted to increase by .21 points, while holding all other predictor variables constant. With a .19 standardized partial regression coefficient, the pay facet score was the least significant of the three significant predictors within the model.

The research study results indicated the combined composite of the areas of people, work, pay, supervision, and opportunities for promotion were related to the job satisfaction of public school-based speech-language pathologists. Work, supervision, and pay explained a statistically significant amount of difference in the JIG job satisfaction score for speech-language pathologists. Based on statistical analysis, the people and opportunities for promotion facets were not statistically significant in explaining the amount of variance in the JIG job satisfaction score. The research demonstrated that work had the strongest impact on the JIG job satisfaction score. Supervision had the second strongest, and pay had the least strength of the three significant predictor variables (Boynton & McDaniel, 2020).

Descriptive Data for Significant Job Facets

Based on inferential statistical results of the research study, the significant job facets were *work*, *supervision*, and *pay*. Identification of the specified job facet variables impacting job satisfaction offers a discussion platform to investigate further, more specifically the JDI descriptors of each facet combined with data related to the percentage of surveyed Indiana, USA, speech-language pathologists responding "Yes," "No," or ? for each facet descriptor. Data are organized based on strength of impact as determined by research study results. The following Tables 5.1–Table 5.12 provide additional detailed information about the individual significant facets, including work, supervision, and pay, and the accompanying percentages for each descriptor. Additionally, data includes a breakdown of each significant facet based on years of clinical experience, an additional variable that will be discussed in Chapter 6.

Work

Table 5.1 Percentage for JDI Descriptors of Work (Less Than Five Years)

Descriptor	Yes	No	?
Fascinating	76.2%	19.0%	4.8%
Routine	71.4%	28.6%	0.0%
Satisfying	95.2%	4.8%	0.0%
Boring	4.8%	95.2%	0.0%
Good	90.5%	0.0%	9.5%
Sense of accomplishment	90.5%	9.5%	0.0%
Respected	57.1%	28.6%	14.3%
Exciting	71.4%	19.0%	9.5%
Rewarding	100.0%	0.0%	0.0%
Useful	95.2%	0.0%	4.8%
Challenging	95.2%	4.8%	0.0%
Simple	9.5%	85.7%	4.8%
Repetitive	61.9%	38.1%	0.0%
Creative	71.4%	23.8%	4.8%
Dull	4.8%	95.2%	0.0%
Uninteresting	0.0%	100.0%	0.0%
Can see results	90.5%	4.8%	4.8%
Uses my ability	100.0%	0.0%	0.0%

Table 5.2 Percentage for JDI Descriptors of Work (Six to Ten Years)

Descriptor	Yes	No	?
Fascinating	43.8%	42.8%	12.5%
Routine	68.8%	25.0%	6.3%
Satisfying	68.8%	25.0%	6.3%
Boring	12.5%	75.0%	12.5%
Good	93.8%	6.3%	0.0%
Sense of accomplishment	81.3%	18.8%	0.0%
Respected	62.5%	25.0%	12.5%
Exciting	37.5%	50.0%	12.5%
Rewarding	93.8%	6.3%	0.0%
Useful	87.5%	6.3%	6.3%
Challenging	87.5%	12.5%	0.0%
Simple	18.8%	75.0%	6.3%
Repetitive	43.8%	43.8%	12.5%
Creative	62.5%	31.3%	6.3%
Dull	12.5%	81.3%	6.3%
Uninteresting	18.8%	75.0%	6.3%
Can see results	75.0%	12.5%	12.5%
Uses my ability	87.5%	12.5%	0.0%

Table 5.3 Percentage for JDI Descriptors of Work (10 to 20 Years)

Descriptor	Yes	No	?
Fascinating	37.5%	33.3%	29.2%
Routine	54.2%	29.2%	16.7%
Satisfying	75.0%	16.7%	8.3%
Boring	16.7%	79.2%	4.2%
Good	83.3%	4.2%	12.5%
Sense of accomplishment	79.2%	12.5%	8.3%
Respected	50.0%	33.3%	16.7%
Exciting	37.5%	37.5%	25.0%
Rewarding	75.0%	16.7%	8.3%
Useful	91.7%	4.2%	4.2%
Challenging	66.7%	20.8%	12.5%
Simple	16.7%	75.0%	8.3%
Repetitive	54.2%	37.5%	8.3%
Creative	70.8%	16.7%	12.5%
Dull	8.3%	91.7%	0.0%
Uninteresting	8.3%	91.7%	0.0%
Can see results	75.0%	12.5%	12.5%
Uses my ability	66.7%	16.7%	16.7%

Table 5.4 Percentage for JDI Descriptors of Work (21 or More Years)

Descriptor	Yes	No	?
Fascinating	66.7%	33.3%	0.0%
Routine	70.0%	30.0%	0.0%
Satisfying	90.0%	3.3%	6.7%
Boring	10.0%	80.0%	10.0%
Good	96.7%	3.3%	0.0%
Sense of accomplishment	93.3%	3.3%	3.3%
Respected	50.0%	30.0%	20.0%
Exciting	53.3%	30.0%	16.7%
Rewarding	100.0%	0.0%	0.0%
Useful	100.0%	0.0%	0.0%
Challenging	96.7%	3.3%	0.0%
Simple	13.3%	83.3%	3.3%
Repetitive	56.7%	36.7%	6.7%
Creative	86.7%	10.0%	3.3%
Dull	13.3%	83.3%	3.3%
Uninteresting	0.0%	100.0%	0.0%
Can see results	96.7%	0.0%	3.3%
Uses my ability	96.7%	3.3%	0.0%

Supervision

Table 5.5 Percentage for JDI Descriptors of Supervision (Less Than Five Years)

Descriptor	Yes	No	?
Supportive	90.5%	9.5%	0.0%
Hard to please	4.8%	95.2%	0.0%
Impolite	4.8%	95.2%	0.0%
Praises good work	81.0%	19.0%	0.0%
Tactful	81.0%	19.0%	0.0%
Influential	66.7%	28.6%	4.8%
Up to date	61.9%	28.6%	9.5%
Unkind	0.0%	100.0%	0.0%
Has favorites	33.3%	66.7%	0.0%
Tells me where I stand	61.9%	28.6%	9.5%
Annoying	0.0%	100.0%	0.0%
Stubborn	4.8%	95.2%	0.0%
Knows the job well	66.7%	28.6%	4.8%
Bad	4.8%	95.2%	0.0%
Intelligent	90.5%	9.5%	0.0%
Poor planner	14.3%	85.7%	0.0%
Around when needed	76.2%	14.3%	9.5%
Lazy	0.0%	95.2%	4.8%

Table 5.6 Percentage for JDI Descriptors of Supervision (Six to Ten Years)

Descriptor	Yes	No	?
Supportive	75.0%	18.8%	6.3%
Hard to please	6.3%	81.3%	12.5%
Impolite	0.0%	93.8%	6.3%
Praises good work	68.8%	31.3%	0.0%
Tactful	87.5%	12.5%	0.0%
Influential	62.5%	18.8%	18.8%
Up to date	43.8%	37.5%	18.8%
Unkind	6.3%	87.5%	6.3%
Has favorites	31.3%	43.8%	25.0%
Tells me where I stand	31.3%	50.0%	18.8%
Annoying	6.3%	87.5%	6.3%
Stubborn	6.3%	87.5%	6.3%
Knows the job well	56.3%	43.8%	0.0%
Bad	0.0%	93.8%	6.3%
Intelligent	93.8%	6.3%	0.0%
Poor planner	6.3%	87.5%	6.3%
Around when needed	56.3%	18.8%	25.0%
Lazy	0.0%	93.8%	6.3%

Table 5.7 Percentage for JDI Descriptors of Supervision (10 to 20 Years)

Descriptor	Yes	No	?
Supportive	66.7%	25.0%	8.3%
Hard to please	8.3%	87.5%	4.2%
Impolite	4.2%	91.7%	4.2%
Praises good work	66.7%	20.8%	12.5%
Tactful	75.0%	16.7%	8.3%
Influential	37.5%	50.0%	12.5%
Up to date	41.7%	41.7%	16.7%
Unkind	4.2%	95.8%	0.0%
Has favorites	54.2%	41.7%	4.2%
Tells me where I stand	62.5%	29.2%	8.3%
Annoying	16.7%	79.2%	4.2%
Stubborn	29.2%	62.5%	8.3%
Knows the job well	29.2%	50.0%	20.8%
Bad	4.2%	87.5%	8.3%
Intelligent	79.2%	4.2%	16.7%
Poor planner	33.3%	66.7%	0.0%
Around when needed	41.7%	37.5%	20.8%
Lazy	4.2%	87.5%	8.3%

Table 5.8 Percentage for JDI Descriptors of Supervision (21 or More Years)

Descriptor	Yes	No	?
Supportive	66.7%	20.0%	13.3%
Hard to please	20.0%	66.7%	13.3%
Impolite	6.7%	86.7%	6.7%
Praises good work	56.7%	33.3%	10.0%
Tactful	73.3%	10.0%	16.7%
Influential	40.0%	33.3%	26.7%
Up to date	33.3%	50.0%	16.7%
Unkind	6.7%	83.3%	10.0%
Has favorites	43.3%	46.7%	10.0%
Tells me where I stand	56.7%	30.0%	13.3%
Annoying	20.0%	66.7%	13.3%
Stubborn	6.7%	80.0%	10.0%
Knows the job well	36.7%	50.0%	13.3%
Bad	0.0%	93.3%	6.7%
Intelligent	76.7%	10.0%	13.3%
Poor planner	20.0%	73.3%	6.7%
Around when needed	56.7%	23.3%	20.0%
Lazy	3.3%	86.7%	10.0%

Pay

Table 5.9 Percentage for JDI Descriptors of Pay (Less Than Five Years)

Descriptor	Yes	No	?
Adequate for normal expenses	52.4%	42.9%	4.8%
Fair	19.0%	71.4%	9.5%
Barely live on income	33.3%	66.7%	0.0%
Bad	47.6%	47.6%	4.8%
Comfortable	38.1%	57.1%	4.8%
Less than I deserve	95.2%	4.8%	0.0%
Well paid	4.2%	95.2%	0.0%
Enough to live on	66.7%	23.8%	9.5%
Underpaid	90.5%	9.5%	0.0%

Table 5.10 Percentage for JDI Descriptors of Pay (Six to Ten Years)

Descriptor	Yes	No	?
Adequate for normal expenses	50.0%	50.0%	0.0%
Fair	31.3%	62.5%	6.3%
Barely live on income	31.3%	62.5%	6.3%
Bad	43.8%	50.0%	6.3%
Comfortable	31.3%	68.8%	0.0%
Less than I deserve	81.3%	12.5%	6.3%
Well paid	6.3%	81.3%	12.5%
Enough to live on	68.8%	25.0%	6.3%
Underpaid	81.3%	12.5%	6.3%

Table 5.11 Percentage for JDI Descriptors of Pay (10 to 20 Years)

Descriptor	Yes	No	?
Adequate for normal expenses	41.7%	54.2%	4.2%
Fair	12.5%	75.0%	12.5%
Barely live on income	37.5%	54.2%	8.3%
Bad	37.5%	50.0%	12.5%
Comfortable	37.5%	58.3%	4.2%
Less than I deserve	91.7%	4.2%	4.2%
Well paid	0.0%	91.7%	8.3%
Enough to live on	54.2%	45.8%	0.0%
Underpaid	87.5%	8.3%	4.2%

Table 5.12 Percentage for JDI Descriptors of Pay (21 or More Years)

Descriptor	Yes	No	?
Adequate for normal expenses	46.7%	50.0%	3.3%
Fair	26.7%	63.3%	10.0%
Barely live on income	36.7%	60.0%	3.3%
Bad	33.3%	53.3%	13.3%
Comfortable	40.0%	46.7%	13.3%
Less than I deserve	73.3%	23.3%	3.3%
Well paid	6.7%	83.3%	10.0%
Enough to live on	53.3%	43.3%	3.3%
Underpaid	73.3%	26.7%	0.0%

In analyzing the results of this study, it is important to revisit that job stress and burnout, as previously discussed, may contribute to recruitment shortages and high attrition of school-based speech-language pathologists. The speech-language pathology field continues to expand into new areas of interest, diagnostics, and intervention. Given the field's continued growth and advancement, career counseling and decision-making are becoming increasingly challenging (Leonard et al., 2016). Understanding the motivations, expectations, and desired outcomes of student clinicians, in addition to reducing current school-based speech-language pathologist stress and burnout, as well as improving perceptions of various aspects of the career, may improve recruitment and retention of current and future school-based speech-language pathologists.

As we explore the descriptive perceptions of each of the research study's job facets, it is important to note the potential impact of professional contacts in the field of speech-language pathology, professors, clinical educators, and personal associations with school-based speech-language pathologists, which may in fact have the potential to support or diminish recruitment and retention efforts for educational settings. Consider the speech-language pathology graduate student completing a clinical practicum placement in a school environment with a highly competent, enthusiastic, licensed and credentialed speech-language pathologist who models continued professional growth and research of evidence-based practice to support students, as well as demonstrates ways to effectively collaborate with teachers and educational colleagues. The student may experience feelings of excitement and future work fulfillment while participating in this clinical practicum placement. Does this scenario guarantee the future speech-language pathologist will find school-based speech-language pathology to be the best fit and pursue a school-based job? Of course not; we can't guarantee our recruitment and retention efforts. Given the many job opportunities in the field and each individual's goals and areas of interest, there is no guarantee; however, it could result in a highly qualified and excited employee joining your school-based team. Consider the potential positive impact on a student who is undecided, but has a wonderful and rewarding clinical practicum experience, resulting in a decision to explore and pursue school-based practice opportunities. Additionally, consider the potential positive impact of an educational leader taking the time to meet and talk with the clinical practicum student about opportunities for future employment. A brief introduction and simple conversation about the current student's interests, goals, and motivations may result in a future committed employee who feels valued from the beginning of his or her experience with your district or cooperative. Time is a challenging aspect of all administrative positions, but taking time to show value and appreciation to possible new and experienced speech-language pathology employees has the potential to support a future payoff resulting in solid recruitment efforts and long-term retention. Investment of this time has the potential to offer valuable time saved if the speech-language pathologist becomes an important member of your educational team. Let's also think about the wider potential of the power of speech-language pathologists who offer help in recruiting new speech-language pathology members for the team.

Organizational Culture

Additionally, exploration of facet-based job satisfaction prompts and encourages a discussion of organizational culture related to job satisfaction when analyzing the results of the study. This study investigated perceptions and attitudes felt about specific job facets. Organizational culture consists of employee attitudes and behaviors impacting the performance and overall well-being of the organization (Belias & Koustelios, 2014). Warr (1992) stated that two characteristics show an organization's overall well-being: the way it functions and the quality of the organization as viewed by its employees. Perceptions, values, beliefs, and insights can't be minimized if we want to ensure an optimal culture promoting job satisfaction that supports solid recruitment and retention. Gaining knowledge about individual and collective group perceptions can offer administrators an opportunity to navigate, reflect, and problem-solve ways to maintain or improve organizational culture. Minimizing the importance of organizational culture will not serve us well in recruitment and retention discussions. Valuable information can be gained by considering perceptual trends, knowledge of barriers, and employee motivation. Organizational culture affects job satisfaction because organizational culture depends on employees' beliefs about the work environment, colleague interactions and relationships, pay, and opportunities for advancement (Belias & Koustelios, 2014). Definitions of organizational culture vary, but common components exist. In all definitions, organizational culture develops in groups with a component of sharing. School environments provide an excellent platform for collaborative work and shared responsibilities. When considering ways to support group culture, one key factor is assurance that all members are included and experience a defined role and are provided an avenue to meaningfully contribute to the work. Once again, time is often a barrier; however, administrators who actively engage and understand the culture within the shared group can support the work, show appreciation for the individual and collective team members, and infuse the desired organizational culture components. It is difficult to deny the complexity of organizational culture; however, the value of exploring the facets, combined with intentional work to collectively develop and nurture positive organizational culture, has the potential to support recruitment and retention efforts, as well as the important consideration of employees with sustained job satisfaction.

Hofstede (1991) emphasized that personal values, generally determined during interactions with family during early development, influence employee behavior within the work environment. This is an interesting and thought-provoking concept to consider because some of the identified factors are most likely developed long before an employee joins an organization; however, they factor into perceptions, actions, and reactions to various organizational scenarios, and ultimately have the potential to impact the culture of an organization. Three cultures influence behavior, including *national culture*, or individual values; *occupational culture*, or perceptions and goals acquired during educational years and professional life experiences; and *organizational culture*, or occupational relationships with colleagues (Hofstede, 1991). If we pause to consider the role each of these cultural influences may play within the development and growth of organizational culture, we begin to see the importance of actively listening to employees and supporting the authentic and meaningful of organizational culture, including all stakeholders. We also must consider the impact of high attrition rates on the ability of an organization to build a sustained culture based on the shared development and communication of perceptions, goals, and values.

Coworker Social Support

Workplace social support from coworkers affects job satisfaction. Harris, Winskowski, and Engdahl (2007) stated workplace collegial support encompasses various interpersonal interactions between colleagues and improves psychological and behavioral performance. Four categories of workplace colleague support are *work support, mentoring, job coaching,* and *coworker support* (Hill, Bahniuk, Dobos, & Rouner, 1989). It seems appropriate to discuss the Clinical Fellowship Year (CFY) and early career speech-language pathologists at this point of the discussion. It is reasonable to consider the potential positive impact of developing and maintaining collaborative opportunities during the early career years. Connections to coworkers within an organization has the potential to support retention efforts. Ensuring early career speech-language pathologists are supported in making coworker connections, as well as including them on grade level, department, and district teams, offers an opportunity to connect with colleagues, develop a deeper understanding of the organization, and support professional growth.

Leadership

Speech-language pathologists employed by public schools experience multiple levels of leadership, including the immediate supervisor or principal of the assigned school and potentially the district special education director or speech-language pathology supervisor. Leaders affect the motivation and satisfaction of those they lead. Motivating factors linked to intrinsic aspects include achievement, opportunity for promotion, recognition of work, and level of responsibility. In contrast, the dissatisfying factors are linked to extrinsic aspects, including working conditions, policies and procedures, pay, supervision, and relationships (Dinham & Scott, 1998). Heller, Clay, and Perkins (1993) stated schools must increase focus on teacher job satisfaction within schools. Since speech-language pathologists share a work environment and leadership with teachers, it is reasonable to consider potential similarities between the two when discussing job satisfaction. School leaders affect job satisfaction in the way they make decisions. Leaders make decisions in one of four ways: making the decision without gaining input, gaining input but determining the final decision, working collaboratively with a group to make a final decision, and sharing the decision-making responsibility with individuals or the collective group (Bogler, 2001). Teachers report increased satisfaction with their work when their leader shares information, communicates, and shares authority (Bogler, 2001). Decreased teacher involvement in the decision-making process results in lower job satisfaction related to the work (Rice & Schneider, 1994). The research indicated teachers and public school-based speech-language pathologists will be positively or negatively impacted by the leadership provided, dependent upon the leader's decision-making approach.

Recruitment and Retention

Job stress and burnout, as previously discussed, may contribute to recruitment shortages and high attrition of school-based speech-language pathologists. The speech-language pathology field continues to expand into new areas of interest, diagnostics, and intervention. Given the field's continued growth and advancement, career counseling and decision-making are becoming increasingly challenging (Leonard et al., 2016). Understanding the motivations, expectations, and desired outcomes of student clinicians, in addition to reducing current school-based speech-language pathologist stress and burnout, may improve recruitment and retention of current and future school-based speech-language pathologists.

Rockwood and Madison (1993) found that students choose careers in speech-language pathology primarily to help people. In addition, the researchers identified six factors as influential to the decision, including job availability, professional contacts, participation in introductory courses, professor contact, career counseling, and career information from brochures or posters (Rockwood & Madison, 1993). Professional contacts and professors with school-based experience may have the potential to support recruitment efforts for educational settings. However, professors or professional contacts with less than desirable school-based experiences may contribute to graduates choosing healthcare positions over school-based opportunities.

Clinical practicum experiences may influence the attitudes and career choices of students in a positive or negative manner depending on the experience. Although positive experiences may not be essential to a student's decision, negative interactions with a mentor may alter a student's preferences and decisions. Mentors described as negative influences possessed three characteristics: professional dissatisfaction, challenging personalities, and poor interactions with clients (Mutha, Takayama, & O'Neil, 1997). Understanding the impact these experiences can have on the development of student preferences and decisions, it is beneficial to consider how we choose mentors for clinical practicum students, CFY, and early career speech-language pathologists. Of course, we want to ensure realistic and accurate experiences, but providing individuals with a positive experience has the potential to positively impact recruitment and retention efforts within school environments.

Perhaps these findings provide insight into the motivating factors of school-based speech-language pathologists. Sahlberg (2011) stated that teachers in Finland find satisfaction in working with people and helping them. Additionally, pay is not the main motivator for working as a teacher in Finland. Analyzing the results of this research led to supporting evidence suggesting the nature of the work of the school-based speech-language pathologist promotes a positive impact on job satisfaction, potentially due to the desire to help people and support the learning, development, and success of children. In considering the role of the work facet, we begin to understand the value of ensuring speech-language pathologists find satisfaction in the work roles and responsibilities. It becomes relevant to highlight that pay was identified as a significant facet, but was not identified as the most significant facet related to overall job satisfaction in this research study. Although pay is a significant factor, there appears to be supporting evidence for contributing intrinsic motivation based on the facet of work.

It is also important to analyze the impact of supervision as a significant facet related to overall job satisfaction. Pink (2009) asserted the importance of positive and useful feedback. It is important to consider feedback based on effort and strategic implementation compared to feedback based on rewards. School leaders may benefit from ensuring speech-language pathologists feel school leaders are accessible, supportive, and understanding of the speech-language pathologists' roles and responsibilities regarding assessment and intervention. Special education directors and principals supervising speech-language pathologists can benefit from learning about the specific roles and responsibilities of these professionals and determine practical, efficient, and meaningful ways to engage them in collaborative curriculum discussion. Although awareness has advanced in recent years, speech-language pathologists continue to experience the need to educate colleagues, parents, and the wider community about their role linked to curriculum and student education. In order to effectively provide optimal services to students and work collaboratively with educational colleagues, speech-language pathologists no longer work in isolation. Integrated and contextualized intervention, tiered intervention supports, and collaborative data analysis are integral components of the speech-language pathologist's roles and responsibilities, ultimately supporting the educational success of students. Breaking down silos continues to be a challenge and brings an increased need for supervisory support. Education leaders without a background in the field of speech-language pathology may determine that it is beneficial to identify a speech-language pathology team leader to maintain and inform the school leader of professional practice changes and best practices.

Significant Facet Analysis and Summary

The analysis of whole sample of data survey results outlined in this chapter provided evidence of a pleasant feeling associated with the speech-language pathology job in schools. Respondents reported the job is worthwhile (85.7%) and provides a sense of accomplishment (86.8%). Robinson (2009) discussed being in "the Element" and suggested when individuals are engaged in something they enjoy and are good at, they feel true to their authentic selves. Given this explanation, it is plausible to consider the possibility that speech-language pathologists associate positive attributes with their work because they are engaged in a job they find fulfilling. It is important for school leaders to understand this need to enjoy work. Of course, there will be barriers and challenges, but a solid foundation built upon job fulfillment and satisfaction has the potential to encourage positive perceptions and a strong desire for problem-solving when faced with adverse situations. Understanding the role of job fulfillment offers us the opportunity during the interview process to inquire about the specifics of the type of school environment, population, and age group that would bring the most sense of self to a potential speech-language pathology candidate. Although it is not possible to find perfect placements for each and every speech-language pathologist in every situation, it can be helpful to understand the expectations, motivations, and goals of current and future speech-language pathologists. School leaders may find it beneficial to consider the potential connection between job satisfaction and retention, particularly given the high demand and competitive market for speech-language pathologists.

As expected, pay surfaced as a significant facet associated with job satisfaction. It is not surprising that pay was identified as a significant facet. Pay is an important extrinsic motivator, meeting the basic needs to live a quality life and provide for one's family. Based on the order of significance, this research study provided evidence that participants in the study identified work and supervision as more significant than pay when studying the relationship to general job satisfaction. The importance of this evidence is linked to the potential pay gaps between various practice settings, including schools, hospitals, long-term care facilities, and clinical settings. In many cases, schools offer the least overall salary compensation compared to other practice settings. School leaders and human resource leaders may benefit from ensuring speech-language pathologist candidates understand the benefits of employment within public education, including the annual work schedule, retirement benefits, and hours worked. It is reasonable to wonder if new speech-language pathologists are aware of the best way to compare different settings, benefits, and job offers to make the most informed decision based on more than pay.

Indeed, supervision was a significant facet identified by the surveyed speech-language pathologists, indicating that a discussion of leadership is essential as we explore the impact of various facets on recruitment and retention in the educational arena. Speech-language pathologists employed by public schools experience multiple levels of leadership, potentially adding complexity to communication with school leaders. Establishing lines of communication between the speech-language pathologist and appropriate school leaders has the potential for supporting increased motivation and satisfaction. School leaders affect job satisfaction in the way they make decisions and lead. It is important to identify and understand the intrinsic and extrinsic motivating factors specific to individual staff members, as well as the overall collective school and district team, to support in developing and sustaining a positive organizational culture. Given the results of the research study identifying work, supervision, and pay as significant facets, we will shift the discussion in Chapter 6 to the investigation of the significance of an additional research variable, years of clinical experience related to general job satisfaction.

Bibliography

Al-Swidi, A., Nawawi, M., & Al-Hosam, A. (2012). Is the relationship between employees' psychological empowerment and employees' job satisfaction contingent on the transformational leadership? A study on the Yemeni Islamic Banks. *Asian Social Science*, *8*(10), 130–150.

American Speech-Language-Hearing Association. (2004). Clinical supervisor's responsibilities. *ASHA Supplement*, *24*, 36–38.

Begley, T., & Czajka, J. (1993). Panel analysis of the moderating effects of commitment on satisfaction, intent to quit and health following organizational change. *Journal of Applied Psychology*, *78*(3), 552–556.

Belias, D., & Koustelios, A. (2014). Organizational culture and job satisfaction: A review. *International Review of Management*, *4*(2), 132–149.

Berry, L. M. (1998). *Psychology at work: An introduction to industrial and organizational psychology*. Boston, MA: McGraw-Hill.

Blood, G. W., Thomas, E. A., Ridenour, J. S., Qualls, C. D., & Hammer, C. S. (2002). Job stress in speech-language pathologists working in rural, suburban, and urban schools: Social support and frequency of interactions. *Contemporary Issues in Communication Science and Disorders*, *29*(2), 132–140.

Bogler, R. (2001). The influence of leadership style on teacher job satisfaction. *Educational Administration Quarterly*, *37*(5), 662–683.

Boynton, K., & McDaniel, T. (2020). Examining job satisfaction through five job facets of public-school speech-language pathologists. *Global Engagement and Transformation*, *4*(1). Retrieved from https://scholarworks.iu.edu/journals/index.php/joget/article/view/29124

Cherrington, D. J. (1994). *Organizational behaviour* (2nd ed.). Boston, MA: Allyn and Bacon.

Coordinating Committee of the Vice President for Speech-Language Pathology Practice. (2009). Role ambiguity and speech-language pathology. *ASHA Leader*, *14*(16), 12–15.

Dinham, S., & Scott, C. (1998). A three domain model of teacher and school executive career satisfaction. *Journal of Educational Research, 75*, 241–247.

Edgar, D. L., & Rosa-Lugo, L. I. (2007). The critical shortage of speech-language pathologists in the public school setting: Features of the work environment that affect recruitment and retention. *Language, Speech, and Hearing Sciences in Schools, 38*, 31–46.

Finn, C. P. (2001). Autonomy: An important component for nurses' job satisfaction. *International Journal of Nursing Studies, 38*(3), 349–357.

Harris, J. I., Winskowski, A. M., & Engdahl, B. E. (2007). Types of workplace social support in the prediction of job satisfaction. *The Career Development Quarterly, 56*, 150–156.

Harris, S. F., Prater, M. A., Dyches, T. T., & Heath, M. A. (2009). Job stress of school-based speech-language pathologists. *Communication Disorders Quarterly, 30*, 103–111.

Heller, H. W., Clay, R., & Perkins, C. (1993). The relationship between teacher job satisfaction and principal leadership style. *Journal of School Leadership, 3*(1), 74–86.

Hill, S. E. K., Bahniuk, M. H., Dobos, J., & Rouner, D. (1989). Mentoring and other communication support in the academic setting. *Group and Organization Studies, 14*, 355–368.

Hofstede, G. (1991). *Culture's consequences: Software of the mind.* Beverly Hills, CA: Sage.

Hutchins, T. L., Howard, M., Prelock, P., & Belin, G. (2010). Retention of school-based SLPs: Relationships among caseload size, workload satisfaction, job satisfaction, and best practice. *Communication Disorders Quarterly, 31*, 139–154.

Johns, G. (1988). *Organisational behaviour.* Boston, MA: Scott, Foresman, and Company.

Kaegi, S., Svitich, K., Chambers, L., Bakker, C., & Schneider, P. (2002). Job satisfaction of school speech-language pathologists. *Journal of Speech-Language Pathology and Audiology, 26*, 126–137.

Kinicki, A. J., McKee, F. M., & Wade, K. J. (1996). Annual review, 1991–1995: Occupational health. *Journal of Vocational Behavior, 49*, 190–220.

Leonard, M. V., Plexico, L. W., Plumb, A. M., & Sandage, M. J. (2016). Emerging practice preference of speech-language pathology students. *Contemporary Issues in Communication Science and Disorder, 43*, 285–298.

Mutha, S., Takayama, J. I., & O'Neil, E. H. (1997). Insights into medical students' career choices based on third-and fourth-year students' focus-group discussions. *Academic Medicine, 72*(7), 635–640.

Pezzei, C., & Oratio, A. R. (1991). A multivariate analysis of the job satisfaction of public school speech-language pathologists. *Language, Speech, and Hearing Services in Schools, 22*, 139–146.

Pink, D. (2009). *Drive: The surprising truth about what motivates us.* New York, NY: Riverhead Books.

Potter, R. E., & Lagace, P. (1995). The incidence of professional burnout among Canadian speech-language pathologists. *Journal of Speech-Language Pathology and Audiology, 19*, 181–186.

Randolph, D. S. (2005). Predicting the effect of extrinsic and intrinsic job satisfaction factors on recruitment and retention of rehabilitation professionals. *Journal of Healthcare Management, 50*(1), 49–60.

Rice, E. M., & Schneider, G. T. (1994). A decade of teacher empowerment: An empirical analysis of teacher involvement in decision-making, 1980–1991. *Journal of Educational Administration, 32*(1), 43–58.

Robinson, K. (2009). *The element: How finding your passion changes everything.* New York, NY: Penguin Group.

Rockwood, G. Z., & Madison, C. L. (1993). A survey of program selection and expectations of current and prospective graduate students. *National Student Speech Language Hearing Association Journal, 20,* 88–98.

Sahlberg, P. (2011). *Finnish lessons: What can the world learn from educational change in Finland?* New York, NY: Columbia University Teachers College.

Suma, S., & Lesha, J. (2013). Job satisfaction and organizational commitment: The case of Shkodra municipality. *European Scientific Journal, 9*(17), 41–51.

Vroom, V. H. (1964). *Work and motivation.* New York, NY: Wiley.

Warr, P. B. (1992). Age and occupational well-being. *Psychology and Aging, 7*(1), 37–45.

Wisniewski, L., & Gargiulo, R. (1997). Occupational stress and burnout among special educators: A review of the literature. *The Journal of Special Education, 31,* 325–346.

Zingeser, L. (2004). Career and job satisfaction. *The ASHA Leader, 9,* 4–13.

6 Professional Experience and Job Satisfaction

Chapter Overview

Chapter 6, "Professional Experience and Job Satisfaction," investigates the second focus in this research study specific to the differences in general job satisfaction among four subgroups based on years of clinical experience. Significance in general job satisfaction was found between speech-language pathologists with 10 to 20 years of clinical experience and those with 21 or more years of experience. Speech-language pathologists with 10 to 20 years of clinical experience indicated significantly lower levels of job satisfaction than did the subgroup with 21 or more years of clinical experience. Additionally, this chapter highlights the benefit of school leaders understanding ways to support the speech-language pathologist with professional growth and collaboration opportunities.

***

The remaining research question included in this research study examined whether the facets, including people, work, pay, supervision, and opportunities for promotion, explained a statistically significant difference in job satisfaction measured by the JDI facets and JIG based on years of experience. A one-way ANOVA statistical test was completed to determine if there was a significant difference in any of the specified facets or JIG scores based on the respondents' years of experience. The assumptions of the one-way ANOVA statistical test were examined, including normality and homogeneity of variance, for each individual facet to ensure all assumptions were met or corrections were made if violations occurred. The assumption of normality was met with a non-significant Shapiro–Wilk test for all levels of the independent variable among the six different dependent variable scores tested. Homogeneity of variance was met for five of the six predictor variables. Homogeneity of variance was violated for the work facet, $F(3, 87) = 5.82$, $p = .001$. Due to this violation, the one-way ANOVA test was significant for the work facet dependent variable, and the Games-Howell post hoc test was utilized since it does not assume equal variances on the dependent variable. There was not a significant difference among job satisfaction in any of the subgroups for people, work, pay, opportunities for promotion, and supervision.

The one-way ANOVA test was significant for the JIG facet, $F(3, 87) = 2.98$, $p = .036$. Due to the significance of the JIG facet and given that the homogeneity of variance was not violated, a Tukey HSD post hoc comparison was conducted to examine the differences among the years of experience subgroups. Tukey HSD post hoc comparisons indicated the 21 or more years of experience subgroup scored the JIG facet significantly higher than the 10 to 20 years' experience subgroup, with $p = .045$.

This research study found significance in general job satisfaction between speech-language pathologists with 10 to 20 years of clinical experience and those with 21 or more years of experience. Speech-language pathologists with 10 to 20 years of clinical experience indicated significantly lower levels of job satisfaction than did the subgroup with 21 or more years of clinical experience. No significance was determined in overall job satisfaction within or between public school-based speech-language pathologists for the subgroups with less than five years and six to ten years of experience. No evidence of significant difference for any additional facets within or between any of the four years-of-experience subgroups were present in the results. These research study results lead to the inquiry of determining the potential reason for the significant variation in job satisfaction between these identified cohorts, as well as critical-thinking and problem-solving opportunities to identify, develop, and implement ways to provide positive impact and support speech-language pathologists at various career stages to develop and sustain high levels of job satisfaction.

Generational Theory

Analysis of the research findings drives the exploration of the theoretical constructs linked to the investigation of job satisfaction variation between cohort groups. Individuals sharing similar social and historical events of the time period they grew up in may share attitudes and behaviors that are often conveyed in the work environment (Andrade & Westover, 2018). Although trends and generalizations may be helpful during analysis of behaviors and attitudes linked to age cohorts, it is also important to ensure awareness of both individual and collective similarities and differences. Maintaining awareness of the collective generational actions, reactions, and responses, combined with identification of individual preferences, behaviors, and attitudes, provides a balanced approach to ensure that generalizations don't

Experience and Job Satisfaction 79

result in incorrect assumptions. It is interesting to note that research of job satisfaction across generations has not led to the variation one might expect. An even more important consideration includes the knowledge that it is challenging to identify and measure generational differences in relationship to job satisfaction with accuracy because several other variables are influential contributors. Additionally, research on generations often focuses specifically on age cohorts, which may or may not support completely accurate results. Consider the speech-language pathologist who transitioned to a career in the field of speech-language pathology at a later stage in life, took time off at various points in the career trajectory, had another career prior to entering the field of speech-language pathology, or practiced in various settings along an individual career path. Do these variables impact the accuracy of the study of generations? Perhaps, but at a minimum, it is valuable to identify and maintain awareness of these potential influential factors. It is valuable to consider the research of age cohorts and generational research, but we should remain cautious of limiting our knowledge base to this narrow path of inquiry. It is a component, but is likely unable to provide a full picture of variations in job satisfaction at various points along an individual's career path. Although it may be valuable to look at the narrow and detailed study of specific factors, it can also offer a benefit to investigate the larger landscape, including the combination of influential factors.

Andrade and Westover (2018) conducted a large-scale global research study investigating variables with impact on job satisfaction when studying age cohorts. The researchers found variables contributing to the variation of job satisfaction across generations included intrinsic and extrinsic rewards, accounting for 20–25% variation; work relations, also contributing to 20–25% variation; and work-life balance, accounting for 8% variation. The identified variables align with the discussion in prior chapters specific to speech-language pathologists, and provide an opportunity for increased depth and breadth of discussion. Work rewards, and work relationships may be linked to organizational culture. Organizational culture can be developed and enhanced through fostering team building, professional learning opportunities, and collaboration at the grade, building, and district levels, supporting a focus on building and sustaining meaningful and valuable work relations. Speech-language pathologists may find satisfaction in opportunities to participate in discussions and collaborative opportunities across grade levels and buildings, as well as to learn and grow with fellow speech-language pathologists within and across districts and practice settings at various points during their career.

Work-life balance is an interesting variable to consider. As a practicing speech-language pathologist recently entering the 21 or more years of experience cohort, I have paused to reflect on my own personal job satisfaction. It has been particularly relevant because of my career-long interest in job satisfaction of speech-language pathologists in school-based settings, combined with a growing commitment to building solid and sustainable recruitment and retention efforts to remediate the speech-language pathologist shortage experienced in many school-based settings. My passion for this body of research has continued to grow over the course of my career due to a strong desire to work alongside highly competent speech-language pathologists providing optimal, high-quality services to the children served in school-based settings. Additionally, I value the importance of job satisfaction as a component of one's own life fulfillment, but also as a needed component for high-quality job performance and commitment, with the potential to decrease burnout and minimize unhealthy job-related stress.

Reflecting on my initial years as a speech-language pathologist and moving through my career path to my current career point has provided me the opportunity to anecdotally identify my personal alignment to the research findings. Personally, over the course of my career to date, I have found the autonomy to develop a stronger understanding of various service delivery models to be one of the components that most positively impacted my transition to higher levels of job satisfaction. Finding ways to provide speech and language services to students while maintaining a desired work-life balance is not an easy task, but an important one. Moving into a career stage that allows for the individual and personal perception of increased confidence, self-determination, and autonomy has shifted my job satisfaction to a higher level. Continuing to collaborate with fellow educators, researching the growth of the field and evidence-based practice, and finding continued avenues for professional growth and development have undeniably fed my ongoing need to develop and sustain meaningful work relationships, practice and professionally grow with autonomy, as well as find and enhance work-life balance. The question remains, why do other practicing speech-language pathologists perceive and identify with higher levels of job satisfaction when moving from 10 to 20 years of experience into 21 or more years of clinical experience? Although this study only provides information about the job satisfaction variation, it provides an opportunity to engage in discussion about potential contributing factors potentially contributing to the identified variation.

Workplace Feedback

Workplace feedback is a solid starting point for engaging in inquiry and discussion of potentially contributing factors, moving beyond the factor of generational age cohorts. Andrade and Westover (2018) caution us to consider the potential for extrinsic rewards to negatively impact intrinsic rewards, particularly when related to motivation. Self-determination theory provides a platform for a discussion about the impact of three basic human needs that have the potential to impact motivation, including competence, autonomy, and relationships (Deci & Ryan, 2008). Dweck (2006) suggested some individuals in the workplace experience an overwhelming need for constant positive feedback and reassurance as well as demonstrate the potential inability to process constructive criticism. The identified lack of growth mindset of some individuals may contribute to a lower level of job satisfaction compared to individuals who value mistakes, enjoy the learning process, and require less extrinsic reward. Educational leaders need to operate with caution to ensure work is not based on generalizations because each individual brings varying strengths and needs, but it may prove valuable to consider the type of reward linked to an individual's best work performance, as well as consider the desire for collective reward when efforts are collaborative. Additionally, the potential of professional competition and a need to prove one's competence must be considered as a possible driving force linked to a decrease in job satisfaction in the 10-to-20-years of experience subgroup. It is a reasonable consideration that in some cases, speech-language pathologists with 21 or more years of experience have more intrinsic motivation due to fewer perceptions of the need to prove competence in comparison to colleagues with fewer years of experience. In fact, some may experience self-confidence allowing for higher levels of contribution in mentoring or leadership roles at the grade, building, and district levels.

Gruenert and McDaniel (2009) emphasized the impact of a collaborative culture on increasing the strength of weaker teachers, but also cautioned that a toxic culture can decrease the strength of the best teachers. Although this research focused on teachers, speech-language pathologists within the school-based setting are educators who often experience many of the same successes and challenges as their teacher colleagues. Speech-language pathologists can be influenced in similar ways by the school community and culture. In fact, speech-language pathologists often engage in higher levels of collaboration with educators within their school building community than with fellow speech-language pathologist colleagues across a district or cooperative, simply by operating as a single speech-language pathologist professional within a building. Interaction and collaboration with speech-language pathologists may occur on a monthly basis when a team meeting occurs, but often daily collaboration opportunities are found within individual school building communities. Is it possible that a positive and healthy school culture built upon trust, growth mindset principles, and a collaborative foundation could support higher levels of job satisfaction, particularly during the 10 to 20 years of clinical experience career stage? It is important to consider how involved your speech-language pathologist is within your school's community and culture. Ensuring that we don't view involvement as simply more tasks, roles, or responsibilities, but instead, view engagement in meaningful collaborative interactions as paramount to building fulfilling and rewarding opportunities.

School leaders may benefit from beginning or continuing to analyze these perceptions and differences and determining ways to build a growth mindset into the school culture to benefit recruitment, retention, and student learning linked to the roles and responsibilities of speech-language pathologists. To prepare current students for the challenges of life, including the need for determination, persistence when faced with adversity, and intrinsic motivation, school leaders may find continued benefit in building this growth mindset into the school culture and through the staff working collaboratively with each other and with students. Speech-language pathologists are highly involved with student learning, particularly in the areas of speech, language, and literacy connections. They can play a valuable role in infusing a growth mindset and healthy organizational cultural norms into your school community.

Leadership and Decision-Making

Building support for ongoing professional growth, opportunities for leadership, and continued active involvement at the school and system levels may prove beneficial to all speech-language pathologists, regardless of years of experience. Individualization and scaffolded development targeting identified areas of interest can empower speech-language pathologists to gain additional breadth and depth of knowledge as their field changes. Indeed, earlier chapters identified the continued expansion of roles and responsibilities, the increased depth of knowledge needed, and the need for comprehensive ongoing professional growth and development opportunities in the field of speech-language pathology. Educational leaders can provide a platform for active listening, support of professional development ideas and opportunities, and collaborative identification of the speech-language pathologist's role on various school teams. It is important to remember the continuously growing scope of practice when realizing the need to support ongoing professional learning opportunities. Early career speech-language pathologists often bring knowledge of the latest evidence-based practices from their recent coursework. Speech-language pathologists with mid-career experience may offer insight into the changes in the field coupled with ongoing experience in the field. Speech-language pathologists with more years of experience may offer extensive knowledge of the ongoing changes in the field, ideas for supporting new speech-language pathologists, and years of experience working in the field. Consider the combined knowledge, relevancy, and collective positive impact potential a team of speech-language pathologists with varying years of experience can offer within an educational setting. Active listening and collaborative discussion can lead to enhanced and rewarding speech and language services for students and teamwork among educational colleagues, regardless of the speech-language pathologist's years of experience. This information highlights the importance for speech-language pathologist collaboration not only within the individual school building, but also across the educational system. Monthly meetings, ongoing colleague communication, support for participation in state and national level discussions, and professional growth opportunities are important ways to support speech-language pathologists in your school, district, or cooperative.

Job Satisfaction Variation

Although it may continue to be difficult to identify the causes or solutions of job satisfaction variation across years of clinical experience, it warrants awareness, discussion, and continued solution-based thinking. A focus on identifying effective avenues of motivation, authentic platforms for meaningful collaboration with a variety of education colleagues, support of professional development and growth across the individual and collective career trajectories with interdisciplinary opportunities, and allowance for autonomy within the systemic parameters may all offer sustainable ways to increase and maintain levels of job satisfaction across professional cohorts. At a minimum, these considerations demonstrate a desire for awareness, understanding, and appreciation of educators, specifically speech-language pathologists, at various career stages. As we transition into the final chapter of this monograph, we will explore ways to invite, include, and share collaborative ways to engage speech-language pathologists in meaningful interactions and discussions within your individual school and system-wide collaborative opportunities.

Bibliography

Andrade, M. S., & Westover, J. H. (2018). Generational differences in work quality characteristics and job satisfaction. *Evidence-Based HRM, 6*(3), 287–304.

Deci, E. L., & Ryan, R. M. (2008). Self-determination theory: A macrotheory of human motivation, development, and health. *Canadian Psychology/Psychologie canadienne, 49*(3), 182–185.

Dweck, C. (2006). *Mindset: The new psychology of success*. New York, NY: Ballantine Books.

Gruenert, S., & McDaniel, T. (2009). The making of a weak teacher. *The School Administrator, 66*(10), 30–33.

7 Research to Practice
Considerations for Educational Leaders

Chapter Overview

Chapter 7, "Research to Practice: Considerations for Educational Leaders," outlines ideas for beginning or continuing to build upon these discussions related to analyzing the data and using the results to inform practice. In continuing the research-to-practice discussion, school leaders and speech-language pathologists can work together to build a stronger system of support for colleagues and students, including maintaining an up-to-date awareness of changes linked to evidence-based practices, a willingness to understand the roles and responsibilities of speech-language pathologists in relationship to colleagues, and appropriate availability to practicing clinicians when situations require supervisory assistance. Speech-language pathology is a field built upon collaboration, communication for all, and evidence-based intervention. These professionals want to be part of the curriculum and learning discussion to support the language and literacy skills of students. Breaking down potential silos and bridging an avenue for participation and collaboration can open doors that will benefit school teams, student communication, and job satisfaction.

***

As a speech-language pathologist, educator, and researcher, I know the importance the research-to-practice connection offers. It is important for speech-language pathologists to identify and continue learning about growth within the field of speech-language pathology, including scope of practice and evidence-based practices, but also ways to develop and sustain job satisfaction across a career trajectory. Additionally, as an educator, I see the importance of ensuring future speech-language pathologists build a strong basis for using research to inform practice, including research related to the need for personal job satisfaction. Lastly, as a researcher, I see the value of informing the broader community to encourage and engage in discussions to promote increased job satisfaction for speech-language pathologists working within school settings. This chapter outlines ideas for beginning or continuing to build upon these discussions related to analyzing the data and using the results of the outlined research study found within this monograph to inform practice.

Indeed, there is no question that all educators have an important role in providing the best educational experience to all students and supporting academic growth as well as social and emotional development. Speech-language pathologists are no exception to this work within the school-based environment. They strive each day to address the communication needs of students built upon individual student strengths, while supporting areas of deficit to ensure every student has an effective means for communicating. As mentioned earlier in this monograph, ASHA supports communication as a human right for all. Working collaboratively with parents, educational colleagues, and administrators is a fundamental role of the speech-language pathologist when supporting students and families. Speech-language pathologists have a knowledge base to share that is able to work in conjunction with curriculum standards. As a result, working collaboratively to gain knowledge of ways to build intervention into contextualized learning opportunities will promote generalization of skills for optimal support of individual student educational success.

As identified in this research study, work was the most significant facet impacting general job satisfaction. Reflecting on this data point solidifies my passion for the field. While each speech-language pathologist has his or her own reason for pursuing this career, personally, I never tire of the joy of seeing a young toddler say his or her first words, a preschooler using picture communication and signs to state her needs, an elementary school student effectively reading and answering comprehension questions for a social studies assignment, a middle school student solving a math problem because the needed math vocabulary is now understood, or a high school student using an Augmentative and Alternative Communication device to talk and laugh with friends while engaging in meaningful peer interactions. These are only a few examples of the beauty and power of communication that I have been honored to be part of during my career as a speech-language pathologist. It is the work I do that brings about positive job satisfaction. Education leaders can demonstrate value of this important work by developing open and collaborative communication to learn more about the detailed work of speech-language pathologists. As a previous school district administrator, I understand the significant and ongoing time constraints that delay or prevent these conversations; however, based on literature review and this current study, it may benefit us to consider ways to ensure speech-language pathologists are invited to and engaged in school and district curriculum conversations.

Based on projected demand exceeding supply, school leaders will likely be recruiting speech-language pathologists from a competitive market both within and outside the field of education. How can school leaders work to recruit and retain speech-language pathologists? I will offer my ideas in hopes of encouraging you to continue thinking about what would work in your school or district. I am fully aware that we can't lean on a single solution or approach. Each school, district, or cooperative can work to build strong recruitment, along with an accompanying retention plan. School leaders can positively promote available school-based speech-language pathology positions by demonstrating a willingness to understand an individual speech-language pathologist's need for work they find fulfilling, including school culture, population, and roles and responsibilities. Finding ways to determine individual and collective group areas of interest, understand and build competency related to the populations served, and initiate discussions specifically focused on role and responsibility definitions within school teams are important components. Building rapport and demonstrating supervisory support can begin with establishing a collaborative avenue for speech-language pathologists to participate in school- and system-level initiatives, program development and implementation, and focused efforts for language and literacy. Unfortunately, in some cases, speech-language pathologists are not invited to participate in these efforts. The oversight, resulting in a missed invitation to participate, is often not purposeful; however, the school is missing a valuable language and literacy contributor in these instances. Consider the intrinsic reward that may result from an invitation to participate in these discussions and the potential for development or maintenance of job satisfaction. These opportunities to enhance the rewarding work through varied opportunities keeps the work interesting, introduces new perspectives, and encourages continued exploration of evidence-based practice. Even more important, consider the contributions the speech-language pathologist can make to supporting students, impacting their educational success. It would be unfair of me to place all responsibility for this communication on school administrators. Communication is a reciprocal exchange with expression and active listening. Speech-language pathologists certainly know how to communicate. In some instances, a speech-language pathologist may find it necessary or beneficial to approach the school leader to inquire and suggest ways to participate in various collaborative or leadership opportunities. These are excellent opportunities to listen and determine ways for involvement. The benefits to the speech-language pathologist, students, and school building and system can be realized when open and collaborative communication is authentic and ongoing.

Additionally, ensuring to the extent possible that each individual speech-language pathologist is assigned to a school with a team dynamic that builds on the individual's strengths and supports continued professional growth will build alignment of individuals and the collective group in a way that most effectively supports students and the potential for the speech-language pathologist's sustained job satisfaction. Unlike teachers, there is typically only one speech-language pathologist assigned to an individual school building. Although speech-language pathologists collaborate with other educators in their building, it can be challenging and isolating at times to lack a speech-language pathology team with whom to problem-solve on a regular basis. Even if speech-language pathology teams meet one time each month, it can be challenging, particularly for early career clinicians, to access enough ongoing support to reach optimal professional growth and build confidence at the desired rate. Educational leaders can build systems of support, including opportunities for the speech-language pathology team to meet at least once each month, combined with opportunities for cross-building collaboration more frequently. Additional opportunities for observation, problem-solving, and easily accessible references for system policies and procedures may decrease stress, impacting overall job satisfaction. Additionally, ensuring introductions of new speech-language pathologists to those who have more years of experience within the school community can begin to build a support system.

In continuing the research-to-practice discussion, school leaders and speech-language pathologists can work together to build a stronger system of support for colleagues and students, including maintaining an up-to-date awareness of changes linked to evidence-based practices, a willingness to understand the roles and responsibilities of speech-language pathologists in relationship to colleagues, and appropriate availability to practicing clinicians when situations require supervisory assistance. As mentioned previously, collaboration is an essential role of the speech-language pathologist's practice. Providing opportunities for collaborative speech-language pathology practice is a key supporting factor. We discussed breaking down silos earlier in this text and it is well worth bringing this back to the discussion again. There are many opportunities for the speech-language pathologist to participate in collaborative teaching opportunities, data analysis teams, and tiered intervention development, planning, and implementation; however, in some cases, many barriers continue to remain. We are aware that time and scheduling can build barriers in places we hope to build bridges. Are there ways in your school community to support finding time or building opportunities into schedules? Could technology support virtual meetings or cross-building collaborative efforts without travel time? Would it be relevant in your school to utilize a portion of the monthly speech-language pathology team meeting for sharing an evidence-based practice that would support professional growth? Could speech-language pathologists, regardless of career stage, be encouraged and empowered to share new knowledge with their individual school teams?

Building routine opportunities for the speech-language pathologist to be a part of individual school and school system-based teams opens doors for building rapport, sharing speech, language, and literacy evidence-based practice information, and navigating ways to creatively support colleagues and students within the general education classroom. I personally believe the road to improved collaboration starts with conversation and rapport building. The clear path will then lead to the potential development and implementation of strong plans and interventions for the most effective student support with optimal generalized learning outcomes.

Indeed, the work and supervision facets were identified as significant variables impacting job satisfaction. Schools must ensure they are not neglecting an important recruitment and retention tool when they lack a focus on intrinsic needs such as positive supervisory relationships and personal growth opportunities, as well as a job assignment aligning with personal values and professional goals. Speech-language pathology is a field built upon collaboration, effective communication for all, and evidence-based assessment and intervention practice. These professionals want to be part of the curriculum, instruction, and learning discussions to support the acquisition, development, and mastery of speech, language, and literacy skills of students. Breaking down potential silos and bridging an avenue for participation and collaboration can open doors that will benefit school teams, student communication, and job satisfaction.

Recommendations for Future Research

To enhance the findings of this research study, further research is necessary related to school-based speech-language pathologists' job satisfaction, including ways to support improved general job satisfaction, to promote strong recruitment and retention practices. This study did not account for urban and suburban school distinctions and focused only on Indiana, USA. Given the differences that may exist in procedures, practices, roles, and responsibilities between urban and suburban settings, as well as other states and countries, an expanded investigation considering school settings and alternate locations may provide additional specific insights about job satisfaction. Additionally, future research studying facet-based job satisfaction between varying practice settings may highlight overall job satisfaction differences and similarities within and across the clinical environments. Perhaps we may see similarities or, alternatively, differences based on work settings. This research study was focused on and limited to school-based speech-language pathologists practicing in Indiana. The national shortage of speech-language pathologists practicing within public schools indicates a need to expand the study beyond Indiana to additional regional and national studies to determine significant similarities and differences in findings. The scope of practice and the need for school-based speech-language pathologists continue to grow. Identifying the significance of specific job facets may contribute nationally to positively affecting the overall shortage of school-based speech-language pathologists.

Caseload and workload provide an ongoing platform for discussion linked to the practice of school-based speech-language pathologists. Indiana speech-language pathologists provide assessment and intervention services within the confines of significantly high caseloads compared to other states with caseload caps. Future study related to the impact of caseload and workload approaches specific to job satisfaction may lead to important insights for practice preference and the impact of those individual decisions. Additionally, the variation of workload implementation may offer strategies for appropriately meeting student needs using this model of service delivery.

Quantitative research specific to school leaders' perceptions of speech-language pathologist job satisfaction would provide comparative and contributing data for the discussion. The question remains whether school leaders have a true understanding of the general job satisfaction of speech-language pathologists. Additionally, such research may bring to light gaps in understanding and identification of areas of positive perceptions and negative perceptions. Linked to this research is the need for a quantitative study analyzing the knowledge and perception of school leaders associated with the roles and responsibilities of speech-language pathologists. This information may be constructive for school leaders seeking to identify additional ways to include speech-language pathologists in collaborative planning and implementation of strategies related to curriculum and instruction practices. Additionally, research investigating the reasons speech-language pathologists leave the profession may provide insight into ways to strengthen support of current speech-language pathologists for the purpose of retention.

Lastly, research specific to recruitment and retention efforts, procedures, and practices may prove crucial for competing within a competitive market. Research featuring comparisons and contrasts in job satisfaction levels in various practice settings, including specific reasons for the results, may be advantageous to all speech-language pathology employers seeking to understand the most successful ways to recruit and retain professionals. Quantitative and qualitative research may yield an overview, combined with more specific analysis of the intricacies of the recruitment and retention process.

Communication Counts

As a final note for continuing to support current and future speech-language pathologists in your school, take the time to have a conversation. Take a few minutes to ask your speech-language pathologist about his or her workload, opportunities for collegial collaboration, and language intervention ideas. Ask about professional goals and find ways to support progress toward achievement. Take an opportunity to inquire about the individual's perceptions about job roles and responsibilities. Learn more about the speech-language pathologist's participation on intervention teams. As educators, we all strive for the same goal: the individual success of each of our students. Based on projections, school districts in Indiana, USA, and nationally may continue to face speech-language pathologist recruitment and retention challenges, but as professionals we can work collaboratively to effectively support the work and professional growth of all educators. Students need the specialized assessment and intervention offered by skilled and licensed speech-language pathology professionals. Schools can work to continue to determine ways to successfully recruit and retain speech-language pathologists in the competitive market to meet the needs of students in need of speech and/or language assessment and intervention. The value of understanding significant facets, including work, supervision, and pay, provides a platform to begin to explore additional ways to provide ongoing support to speech-language pathologists in school-based settings. The fact remains that effective communication is at the heart of the speech-language pathologist's work: the work that impacts job satisfaction.

Index

Note: Page numbers in **bold** indicate a table on the corresponding page.

Al-Hosam, Asma 48
Al-Swidi, Abdullah Kaid 48
American Speech-Language-Hearing Association (ASHA) 7, 9, 18, 21, 30, 41; broad areas of speech-language pathology, identifying 15; career and job satisfaction, distinguishing between 45; caseload number recommendations 19–20; communication as a human right for all 23, 85; on diverse client population training 17
Andrade, Maureen S. 79, 80–81
ANOVA statistical analysis 43, 60, 77–78
attainment in occupational decision-making model 30
audiology 4, 30
Augmentative and Alternative Communication Device (AAC) 21–22, 85

Bakker, Cynthia 47
Bandura, Albert 31–32
Bedwinek, Anne 29
Belin, Gayle 46
Blenkarn, Katie 21
Blood, Gordon W. 19, 46
Brewer, Brewer B. 5
Byrne, Nicole 33

careers in speech-language pathology 4, 5, 48, 79, 80; career counseling for the field as challenging 6–7;
early career clinicians 31, 33, 49, 70, 71, 82, 87; expectancy theory of motivation 27–30; fixed mindset, career success achieved through 2; job satisfaction vs. career satisfaction 45, 47; social cognitive career theory 32–33
Carson, Kenneth P. 40
caseload approach 7, 18–22, 46–47, 89
Certificate of Clinical Competence in Speech-Language Pathology (CCC-SLP) 9
Chambers, Leslie 47
Ciocci, Sandra R. 4–5
Clay, Rachel 70
Clinical Fellowship Year (CFY) 5, 9, 15, 41, 70, 71
Cocks, Naomi 29
Coordinating Committee of the Vice President for Speech-Language Pathology Practice 15, 47
coworker facet of job satisfaction 5, 29, 69, 70; JDI, measuring workplace satisfaction through 6, 8, 61, 77–78; JIG, calculating job satisfaction via 6, 8, 36–37, 39, 42; in null hypothesis 38, 59; as a predictor variable 37, 42, 59–60; in survey design 39–40, 46; whole sample data analysis findings 49–50, 52, 54, 56, 58
criterion variable 36, 37, 38, 42–43, 59–60

Du, Jinyu 29
Dweck, Carol 2, 81
Dyches, Tina Taylor 46

early intervention 18
Edgar, Debra L. 18, 46
Education for All Handicapped Act 22
Engdahl, Brian E. 70
Every Student Succeeds Act (ESSA) 23
expectancy theory of motivation 27–30, 31

facet-based job satisfaction 4, 8, 11, 36, 43, 45, 48, 68
Fallon, Karen A. 21
feedback 32, 72, 80–82
Finland, teacher satisfaction in 72
Finn, Christine P. 48
free and appropriate public education (FAPE) 22–23
functional communication, goal of 16

Games-Howell post hoc test 77–78
Gargiulo, Richard M. 46
generalization as goal of speech/language intervention 16
general job satisfaction 45, 73, 77, 88, 89; as a criterion variable 36, 37; full- or part-time work as a factor 36, 37; longevity at job as a consideration 74, 78; organizational culture, impact on 44; tools of measurement 6, 40, 60; work as facet most impacting 85; *see also* job satisfaction
general vocational theory 5
generational theory 78–80
Gonzalez, Lori S. 16
growth mindset 2–3, 31, 81–82
Gruenert, Steve W. 81

Hammer, Carol Scheffner 19, 46
Harris, J. Irene 70
Harris, Stephanie Ferney 46
healthcare practice and settings 15, 29, 47, 71, 88
Heath, Melissa Allen 46
Heller, H. William 70
Hird, Kathryn 29
Hofstede, Geert 69

homogeneity of variance 43, 60, 77, 78
homoscedasticity 42
Howard, Malinda 46
Hulin, Charles L. 8, 39
Hutchins, Tiffany L. 46

Indiana Professional Licensing Agency (IPLA) 41
Individual Education Plan (IEP) 7, 19, 23
Individuals with Disabilities Education Act 22–23
instrumentality 28, 29

Job Descriptive Index (JDI) 6, 36, 38, 39, 41; 10 to 20 years, findings for 55–57; 21 years plus, data discoveries 57–59; ANOVA statistical test and 43, 60, 77; defining and describing 8, 40; five years or less, descriptive analysis for 51–53; significant job facets 61, **62, 63, 64, 65, 66, 67**; six to ten years, data on 53–55
job facets *see individual facets of job satisfaction*
Job in General Scale (JIG) 6, 8, 42, 59, 61; ANOVA statistical test and 43, 60, 77–78; global job satisfaction, measuring 37; in survey design 39–41; as a survey tool 36, 38; in whole sample descriptive data 49, 51, 54, 56, 57
job satisfaction: as a dynamic construct 40; effective communication at the heart of 90; future research recommendations 88–89; generational differences in relation to 79; global job satisfaction 8, 36, 37, 39, 47, 48; in nursing/medical field 5–6, 48; *see also* general job satisfaction

Kaegi, Sofie 47
Katz, Lauren A. 21
Kendall, Lorne M. 8, 39
Kinicki, Angelo 40, 44
Kramer, Marlene 5–6

Lagacé, Patricia 47
Language for Learning period 15

leadership in speech-language pathology 7, 15, 45; decision-making of leaders 71, 82–83; educational leaders, defining and describing 18; general job satisfaction, true understanding of 89; healthy work environments, setting tone for 6; job satisfaction, leadership affecting 40, 48, 70; leadership opportunities 10, 82, 86; self-confidence of leaders in field 81
least restrictive environment (LRE) 23
Lent, Robert W. 32–33

Maag, Abby 21
Madison, Charles 71
Maguire, Patricia 5
Matteson, Michael T. 30
McDaniel, Terry M. 81
McKee-Ryan, Frances M. 43, 44
Miller, Suzanne M. 4–5
Morgenroth, Thekla 31
motivational theory of role modeling 27, 30–31
multicollinearity 42, 59
multidisciplinary team-based assessment 15
multiple regression statistical test 42, 59
Multi-tiered Systems of Support (MTSS) 9, 46

Nawawi, Mohd Kamal Mohd 48
Norbury, Courtenay 15
null hypotheses 36, 38, 42, 59

occupational choice 30
occupational culture 68–69
Omnibus Surveys 45, 47
Oratio, Albert R. 45
organizational culture 68–69, 74, 79

Paul, Rhea 15
pay facet of job satisfaction 29, 69, 70, 72, 90; JDI, measuring pay satisfaction via 6, 8, **66**, **67**, 77–78; JIG, calculating wage satisfaction through 6, 8, 37, 42, 60–61; in null hypothesis 38, 59; in Omnibus Survey 47; as a predictor variable 37, 42, 59–60; satisfaction with pay as vital 45, 46, 48, 73, 74; in survey design 39–40; whole sample data analysis findings 49, 50, 52, 54, 56, 58
people facet *see* coworker facet of job satisfaction
Perkins, Cline 70
Peters, Kim 31
Peters-Johnson, Cassandra 20
Pezzei, Carolyn 45
Pink, Daniel 72
Potter, Robert E. 47
Prater, Mary Anne 46
predictor variables *see under individual job facets*
Prelock, Patricia 46
private practice 8, 11, 88
professional growth 2, 45, 49, 67, 80; commitment to the field and 46; early career clinicians, challenges of 87; support for 9–10, 47, 70, 82, 83, 90
promotion facet of job satisfaction 29, 69, 70; JDI as measuring satisfaction with opportunities 6, 8, 77–78; JIG as weighing positive expectations 6, 37, 42, 60–61; in null hypothesis 38, 59; as a predictor variable 37, 42, 59–60; in survey design 39–40, 45; whole sample data analysis findings 49, 50–51, 53, 54–55, 57, 58

Qualls, Constance Dean 19, 46

Randolph, Diane Smith 48
rehabilitation practice and settings 8, 47, 48, 88
Response to Intervention (RTI) 9, 46
retention strategies and recruitment efforts 2, 6, 71–72; contributors to stress and burnout 3, 29; coworker connections as a potential retention tool 70; demand as exceeding supply of clinicians 4, 10–11; research questions on 37–38
Ridenour, Jenna Swavely 19, 46
Robinson, Ken 73
Rockwood, Greta 71
Rosa-Lugo, Linda I. 18, 46
Ryan, Michelle K. 31

Sahlberg, Pasi 72
Schmalenberg, Claudia 5
Schneider, Phyllis 47
Schriesheim, Chester A. 43
self-determination 3, 80, 81
Smith, Brian K. 29
Smith, Megan K. 21
Smith, Patricia Cain 8, 39–40
Smith, Samuel V. 30
social cognitive theory 27, 31–33
special education: Individuals with Disabilities Education Act and 22–23; special education assessment 17, 21; special education cooperatives 11, 37, 38–39, 41; special education directors 70, 72
speech-language pathology, field of: collaboration, as a field built on 88; credentialing process 9–10; definition of terms 7–8; functional communication as true goal of 16; overview 8–9; prior exposure to field as a factor 33; roles and responsibilities 14–18; scope of practice 10–11, 17
Stewart, Sharon R. 16
supervision facet of job satisfaction 15, 69, 72, 88, 90; clinical supervision 10, 29; collaborative working conditions, establishing 86; as an extrinsic factor in job satisfaction 70, 73; JDI, measuring satisfaction with 6, 8, **64**, **65**, 77–78; JIG, revealing positivity towards 6, 37, 42, 60–61, 74; in null hypothesis 38, 59; as a predictor variable 37, 42, 59–60; research-to-practice connections 84, 87; in survey design 39–40, 45; whole sample data analysis findings 49, 51, 53, 55, 57, 58–59
Svitich, Karen 47

team-teaching methodology 23
Thomas, Emily A. 19, 46
tiered interventions 17
transdisciplinary planning 15
Tukey honest significant difference test (Tukey HSD) 43, 78

valence 28, 29
Vroom, Victor 28–30, 31, 44

Wade, Kimberly J. 44
Warr, Peter B. 68
Westover, Jonathan H. 79, 80–81
Whitehouse, Andrew 29
whole sample data analysis 44, 49–59, 73
Winskowski, Ann Marie 70
Wisniewski, Lech 46
work facet of job satisfaction 29, 69, 70, 72, 85; JDI, measuring satisfaction with 6, 8, **62**, **63**, 77; JGI, calculating data through 6, 8, 36–37, 40, 42, 60–61; in null hypothesis 38, 59; as a predictor variable 36, 42, 59–60; in survey design 39–40, 45; whole sample data analysis findings 49, 50, 52, 54, 56, 58
work-life balance 45, 79–80
workload approach 8, 18–22, 48, 89
workplace colleague support, four categories of 70

For Product Safety Concerns and Information please contact our EU
representative GPSR@taylorandfrancis.com
Taylor & Francis Verlag GmbH, Kaufingerstraße 24, 80331 München, Germany

www.ingramcontent.com/pod-product-compliance
Lightning Source LLC
Chambersburg PA
CBHW050843160426
43192CB00011B/2134